1/5 3/18.

Up and Running with Autodesk® Inventor® Professional 2014

PART 1 – Stress and Frame Analysis

Wasim Younis BEng (Hons), MSc CAE, CEng MIMechE, Cert Ed
Autodesk® Authorized Author

DEDICATION

To all the designers and engineers out there who are using Inventor Stress and Frame analysis as part of their design process to help them create innovative products.

CONTENTS

Acknowledgements

I would also like to thank all the companies, mentioned below, for allowing me to use their innovative product designs and models, without which none of this would have been possible.

Ian Parker – Halifax Fan Limited
Lee Chapman – Unipart Rail
Chris Tait - Destec Engineering Ltd
Jonathan Stancliffe – British Waterways
Philip Wright – Wright Resolutions Ltd
Mark Johnson - Variable Message Signs Ltd
Alex Ferguson - Croft Ltd
Adrian Hartley – Simba Great Plains Ltd
Adrian Curtis – In-CAD Services Ltd
Kevin Berry – Triple Eight Race Engineering Ltd
Adrian Oaten – Aerospace Design Facilities Ltd
Carl Geldard – Planet Platforms Ltd
Brian White – KONE plc (Escalators, Keighley)
Stephen Bennett - James Alpe Ltd
Mike Smith - Swire Oilfield Services Ltd

Finally I would like to thank my wife Samina, daughter Malyah and son's Sami and Fasee for their unconditional love, support and source of inspiration.

The front cover image shows an illustration of an Offshore Container used courtesy of Swire Oilfield Services Ltd (http://www.swireos.com/).

About the Author

An Autodesk simulation solutions manager with more than 20 years of experience in the manufacturing field, including working at Rolls Royce, British Aerospace and Nuclear Electric. Has been involved with Autodesk simulation software when it was first introduced, and is well-known throughout the Autodesk Simulation community, worldwide.

He also presents annually at Autodesk University, a prestigious event held annually in USA, including contributing articles, whitepapers, tips and tricks and tutorials to various forums. He authors simulation Tips and Tricks articles on his own Virtual Reality blog - which is completely dedicated to the Autodesk Simulation Community. He also runs a dedicated forum for simulation users on LinkedIn —Up and Running with Autodesk Inventor Simulation

Wasim has a bachelor's degree in mechanical engineering from the University of Bradford and a master's degree in computer- aided-engineering from Staffordshire University.

Currently he is employed @ Symetri (*http://www.symetri.co.uk*) – an Autodesk Manufacturing Platinum partner in UK.

Contact Details:

Email:	younis_wasim@hotmail.com
Blog:	http://vrblog.info/
Support: Forum	http://www.linkedin.com/groups?mostPopular=&gid=2061026

Preface

Welcome to the fifth edition of *Up and Running with Autodesk® Inventor® Professional 2014 – Step by step guide to Engineering Solutions.*

I hope you found the previous editions of my books very useful and interesting. I thank you very much for your feedback/suggestions, which have helped me again to make this edition of the book even better. This edition of the book includes two new design problems, including enhancing several existing design problems.

This book has been written using actual design problems, all of which have greatly benefited from the use of Simulation technology. For each design problem, I have attempted to explain the process of applying Inventor Simulation using a straightforward, step by step approach, and have supported this approach with explanation and tips. At all times, I have tried to anticipate what questions a designer or development engineer would want to ask whilst he or she were performing the task and using Inventor Simulation.

The design problems have been carefully chosen to cover the core aspects and capabilities of Stress and Frame Analysis and their solutions are universal, so you should be able to apply the knowledge quickly to their own design problems with more confidence.

The book basically comprises of six sections: Stress Analysis Environment (Chapter 1), Design Problems using Solid Elements (Chapter 2-6), Design Problems using Thin Elements (Chapter 7-10), Design Problems using Motion Loads (Chapter 11-12), Modal Analysis (Chapter 13) and Frame Analysis (Chapter 14 – 17). Chapters 1 & 14 provide an overview of stress, frame analysis and the Inventor Simulation's interface and features so that you are well-grounded in core concepts and the software's strengths, weaknesses and work around. Each design problem illustrates a different unique approach and demonstrates different key aspects of the software, making it easier for you pick and choose which design problem you want to cover first; therefore, having read chapter 1 and 14, it is not necessary to follow the rest of the book sequentially.

This book is primarily designed for self-paced learning by individuals, but can also be used in an instructor-lead classroom environment.

I hope you will find this book enjoyable and at the same time very beneficial to you and your business. I will be very pleased to receive your feedback, to help me improve future editions. Feel free to email me on ***younis_wasim@hotmail.com***

How to access training files

All tutorial files and datasets necessary to complete the training manual's exercises, plus completed files, and much more, can be accessed from;

1 - http://vrblog.info/

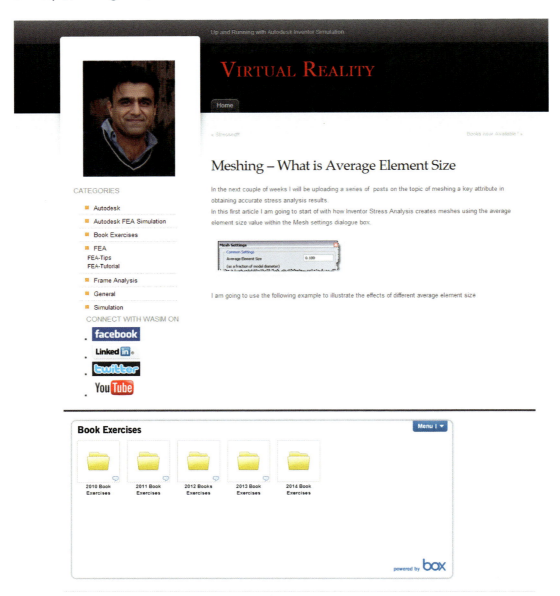

The Book exercises are available on the bottom of the blog page (available on all pages/posts). You may need to scroll-down a little to see the exercise-files available via Box.net
NB: datasets for version 2010, 2011, 2012 2013 and 2014 are available from here

Section 1 - STRESS ANALYSIS *Essentials*

The Stress Analysis Environment

The Finite Element Method (FEM) - An Overview

The finite element method (FEM) is a mathematical/computer-based numerical technique for calculating the strength and behavior of engineering structures. Autodesk Inventor – and much other analysis software - is based on the FEM, where, simply, a component is broken down into many small elements, as shown below.

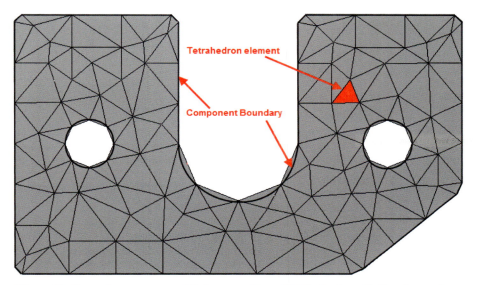

Discretization of a component into a number of Tetrahedron finite elements

Let's assume that we need to determine the displacement of the component. This displacement (unknown quantity) acts over each element in a predefined manner – with the number and type of elements chosen so that overall distribution through the component is sufficiently approximated. This distribution across each element is commonly presented by a polynomial- whether it's linear, quadratic or even cubic. It is important to note FEM is always an approximation of the actual component and is by its very nature will have errors due to discretization - particularly around curved boundaries (as shown above) or geometrically complex components.

These errors due to discretization can be reduced by either specifying more elements or using higher order polynomials to approximate the distribution of the unknown quantity over the elements - also referred to as polynomial interpolation function. Most finite element software uses the former method, specifically known as the H refinement process, in which the software goes through an iterative process of reducing the number of elements at each iteration until the results have converged. The latter method, of using higher order polynomials, is called the P-refinement process, in which the software increases the order of the polynomial at each iteration starting from 1(linear) to 2(quadratic), 3(cubic) and so on.

CHAPTER 1
The Stress Analysis Environment

Another approach to reduce errors due to discretization is to user higher order elements; this is discussed in the next section in more detail.

Types of Finite Element Method (FEM) Elements

Autodesk Inventor Stress Analysis uses first and second order tetrahedron and thin elements, as shown below.

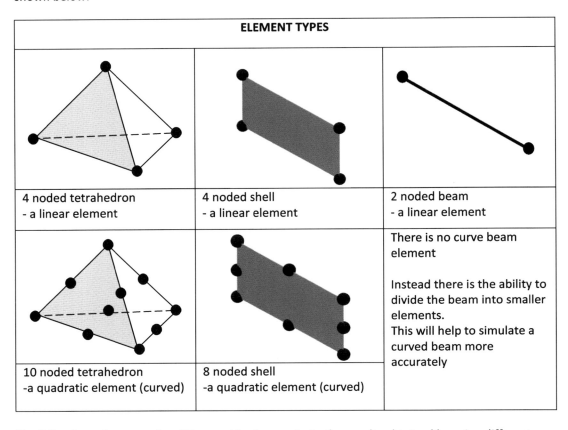

ELEMENT TYPES		
4 noded tetrahedron - a linear element	4 noded shell - a linear element	2 noded beam - a linear element
10 noded tetrahedron -a quadratic element (curved)	8 noded shell -a quadratic element (curved)	There is no curve beam element Instead there is the ability to divide the beam into smaller elements. This will help to simulate a curved beam more accurately

The following tube example will be used to demonstrate the results obtained by using different element types.

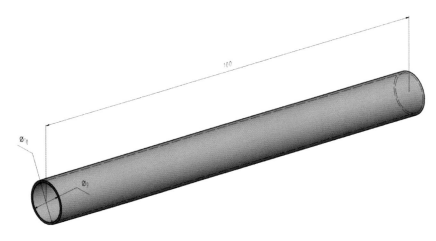

Initially we will determine theoretical results for the tube. We will fix the tube at one end and apply a load of 100N at the other end

Tube data to be used is as follows;

Length   = 100mm
Diameter = 10mm
Thickness = 0.5mm
Material   = Mild Steel

Using the classical Bending Stress Equation:

$$\frac{M}{I} = \frac{\sigma}{y} = \frac{E}{R}$$

we can determine maximum stress (at fixed end)

M_{max} = Total length x Load = 100 x 100 = 10,000Nmm

y = 5mm

$$I = \frac{\pi}{64}(\varnothing_{outside}^{4} - \varnothing_{inside}^{4}) = \frac{\pi}{64}(10^{4} - 9^{4}) = 168.8mm^{4}$$

$$\sigma max = \frac{My}{I} (10000 \ x \ 5)/168.8 \ = \ 296 \ N/mm^{2}$$

 A local mesh refinement of 5mm was used (on all faces in case of tetrahedon elements) for the following stress analysis results.

Stress Analysis Results - using 4 noded tetrahedron elements - 316 N/mm^{2} or (316 MPa)

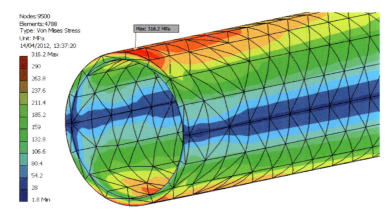

Nodes:9500
Elements:4788
Type: Von Mises Stress
Unit: MPa
14/04/2012, 13:37:20
316.2 Max
290
263.8
237.6
211.4
185.2
159
132.8
106.6
80.4
54.2
28
1.8 Min

Max: 316.2 MPa

% difference = 6.75. Although this value is acceptable (within 10%) the difference is primarily due to stress singularities as refining the mesh around the high stress area will result in higher stresses. This is discussed later in the chapter

CHAPTER 1
The Stress Analysis Environment

Stress Analysis Results - using 4 noded shell elements - 287 N/mm^2

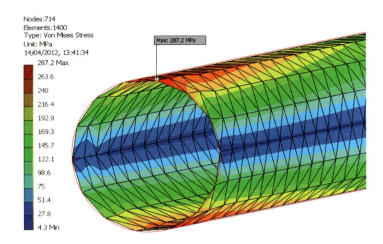

% difference = 3%. This is almost 50% better than using tetrahedron elements.

 Use shell elements for thin structures to get more accurate stress results

Frame Analysis Results - using beam elements - 296 N/mm^2

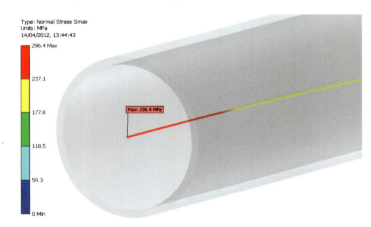

% difference = 0%. This is because frame analysis does not have the stress singularity issues as in stress analysis.

Use beam analysis for structures with a uniform cross section and also have a length/cross section ratio generally above 10.

Frame analysis is discussed in detail in chapters 14-17.

In the next section we will discuss how to improve stress analysis result.

Methods to enhance Finite Element Method (FEM) Results

In summary there are three methods within Autodesk Inventor Simulation that can be used to enhance the accuracy of the results:

1. P-refinement
2. H-refinement
3. Higher order elements

There are pros and cons of using both P- and H-refinement

	H-refinement	P-refinement
Results convergence	Slower – polynomial rate of convergence	Faster – exponential rate of convergence
Analysis time	Faster - in comparison to P-refinement	Slower – especially as P order increases
Stress singularities	Can converge – with careful consideration to settings	Never convergences

 P-refinement is automatically controlled by the software.

 It is worth noting that curved elements can take more time to produce results when compared to linear elements, especially for a large or complex model.

 For complex shapes it is always advisable to use quadratic elements.

 When using quadratic elements it can take twice as long to analyze the results, as compared to linear elements.

The following diagram illustrates that one quadratic element around a 90^0 circular object/component is better than two linear elements, as the quadratic element tries to match the 90^0 arc more closely and also can affect the accuracy of result.

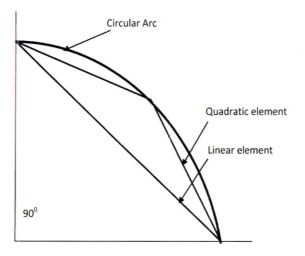

SECTION 1 -Stress Analysis Essentials

Also it is worth noting that the curved element almost matches the true profile of a 45^0 curved object (< 1% geometrical error). Therefore, it is advisable to have at least two quadratic elements around a 90^0 arc, whereas there should be at least three linear elements, preferably four, around a 90^0 circular object.

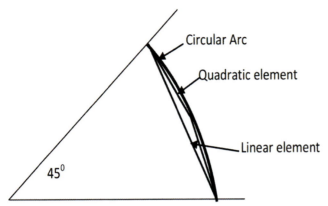

In summary there are three methods within Autodesk Inventor Simulation that can be used to enhance the accuracy of the results:

1. P-refinement
2. H-refinement
3. Higher order elements

There are pros and cons of using both P- and H-refinement

	H-refinement	P-refinement
Results convergence	Slower – polynomial rate of convergence	Faster – exponential rate of convergence
Analysis time	Faster - in comparison to P-refinement	Slower – especially as P order increases
Stress singularities	Can converge – with careful consideration to settings	Never convergences

 P-refinement is automatically controlled by the software.

 It is worth noting that curved elements can take more time to produce results when compared to linear elements, especially for a large or complex model.

 For complex shapes it is always advisable to use quadratic elements.

 When using quadratic elements it can take twice as long to analyze the results, as compared to linear elements.

Autodesk Inventor Simulation overcomes the pros and cons of both method by be using an H-P refinement approach, with some benefits being:

1. Exponential convergence in practical calculations (in cases with stress concentrations and stress singularities).
2. Potential of exponential convergence and maximize sparseness of the stiffness matrix.

Autodesk Inventor Simulation takes this H-P refinement approach one step further by making the H-P approach adaptive. This means that the software will only refine the elements around the high stress areas - rather than the whole model - meaning that the results convergence process will be further enhanced. This process is explained in the next section

H-P convergence

Within Inventor Simulation, the user can only control H-refinement part of the H-P refinement convergence process. The software automatically increases P-order from one to three for every part analysis and from one to two for assembly analysis. The assembly analysis does not use a P-order of three because, as P –order gets higher than two, the analysis time can get exponentially longer - especially when there are a lot of parts to analyze.

If the user has specified two iterations for H-refinement in the Convergence dialogue box, the software will perform the following H-P refinement:

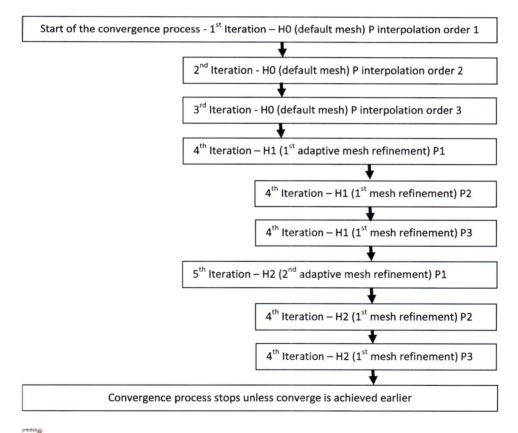

| Start of the convergence process - 1st Iteration – H0 (default mesh) P interpolation order 1 |
| 2nd Iteration - H0 (default mesh) P interpolation order 2 |
| 3rd Iteration - H0 (default mesh) P interpolation order 3 |
| 4th Iteration – H1 (1st adaptive mesh refinement) P1 |
| 4th Iteration – H1 (1st mesh refinement) P2 |
| 4th Iteration – H1 (1st mesh refinement) P3 |
| 5th Iteration – H2 (2nd adaptive mesh refinement) P1 |
| 4th Iteration – H2 (1st mesh refinement) P2 |
| 4th Iteration – H2 (1st mesh refinement) P3 |
| Convergence process stops unless converge is achieved earlier |

This H-P convergence process is very efficient, except when the model does not have stress singularities present. Stress Singularities and methods to overcome them are explained later.

CHAPTER 1
The Stress Analysis Environment
Linear and Nonlinear analysis

Autodesk Inventor Simulation is only capable of performing linear analysis where components have small deformations, under operational loading conditions. On the other hand, nonlinear analysis typically involved when components are experiencing large deformations and thus component material can deform beyond the elastic limit.

Linear analysis

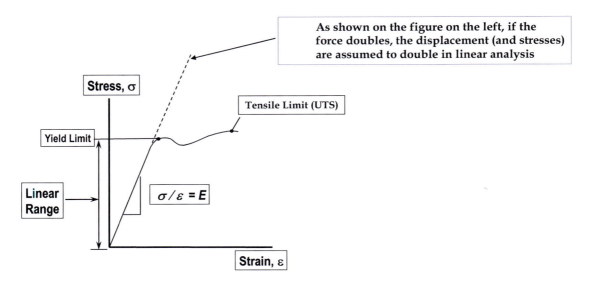

As shown on the figure on the left, if the force doubles, the displacement (and stresses) are assumed to double in linear analysis

Young's Modulus provides the stiffness of the material; for example a higher Young's Modulus will produce a stronger material and a lower Young's Modulus will produce a weaker material.

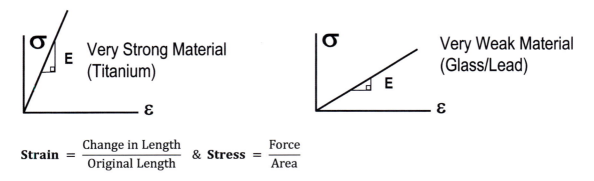

$$\text{Strain} = \frac{\text{Change in Length}}{\text{Original Length}} \quad \& \quad \text{Stress} = \frac{\text{Force}}{\text{Area}}$$

(Note: for linear analysis it is assumed that the change in length is very small compared to the original length.)

Assumptions normally made when conducting a linear analysis
1	The material properties of the component remain linear after the yield limit. Hence, results beyond this limit are not valid using Autodesk Inventor Simulation Suite.
2	The deflections of components are small compared to overall component size.
3	The components are rigid and ductile like metal (not rubber).
4	The components deform equally in all three directions; that is, the material properties are isotropic.

Nonlinear analysis

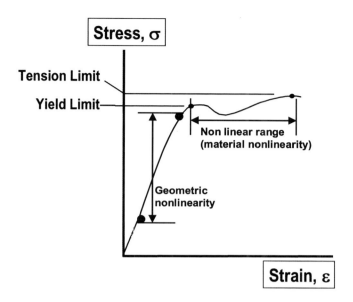

Non-linear Analysis falls into the following three categories;

Geometric nonlinearity – Where a component experiences large deformations and as a result can cause the component to experience nonlinear behavior. A typical example is a fishing rod.

Material nonlinearity – When the component goes beyond the yield limit, the stress/strain relationship becomes nonlinear as the material starts to deform permanently.

Contact – Includes the effect of two components coming into contact; that is, they can experience an abrupt change in stiffness resulting in localized material deformation at region of contact.

Currently, Autodesk Inventor Simulation allows performance of linear static and modal analysis; both are discussed in the next sections.

Static analysis - an overview

Static analysis is an engineering discipline that determines the stress in materials and structures subjected to static or dynamic forces or loads. The aim of the analysis is usually to determine whether the element or collection of elements, usually referred to as a structure or component, can safely withstand the specified forces and loads. This is achieved when the determined stress from the applied force(s) is less than the yield strength the material is known to be able to withstand. This stress relationship is commonly referred to as factor of safety (FOS) and is used in many analyses as an indicator of success or failure in analysis.

$$\textbf{Factor of Safety} = \frac{\text{Yield Stress}}{\text{Calculated Stress}} = \frac{\text{Ultimate Stress}}{\text{Calculated Stress}}$$

Factor of Safety can be based on either Yield or Ultimate stress limit of the material. The factor of safety on yield strength is to prevent detrimental deformations and the factor of safety on ultimate strength aims to prevent collapse, and can only be conducted by nonlinear analysis software.

CHAPTER 1
The Stress Analysis Environment

Autodesk Inventor can only perform linear analysis and hence FOS will more commonly be based on yield limit.

Below are some examples of where static analysis can be useful.

Canal Bridge

The canal bridge is typical example of static analysis. Here, one will be interested to know whether the bridge will withstand a load of a vehicle when it crosses the bridge. This will also help us identify weak spots of the structure, ultimately allowing us design a bridge to carry the maximum physically possible load.

For Halifax Fan we need to be able, for example, to determine the maximum deflection of the blade, which can have an impact on the efficiency of the fan. With the help of static analysis, the blade can be studied and analyzed to reduce deformation, for example by using different materials, increasing the thickness, or adding structural stiffeners.

One of the major obstacles when conducting static analyses is stress singularities, which can significantly distort results and may reduce confidence in the results, as illustrated and discussed in the next section.

Stress singularities

Stress Singularities are a major concern when analyzing results as they considerably distort results. They are also a main cause for non-convergence of results. So, the first question is -what is stress singularity? This can be best explained by the following example.

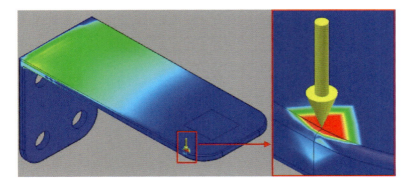

SECTION 1 -Stress Analysis Essentials

This bracket has a localized high stress around the force applied on a point. This stress can be considerably higher than the operational stress and applying a more dense mesh around this simply leads to a much higher stress. This phenomenon is known as stress singularity where the stress becomes infinite, as illustrated by the following formula:

$$\textbf{Stress (infinite)} \; = \; \frac{\text{Force}}{\text{Area of point (almost} = 0)}$$

Therefore, to avoid stress singularities when applying loads, it is recommended **not to apply loads at points and small edges**.

Stress Singularities can also occur **by applying constraints on points and small edges** – even faces with sharp corners as illustrated below.

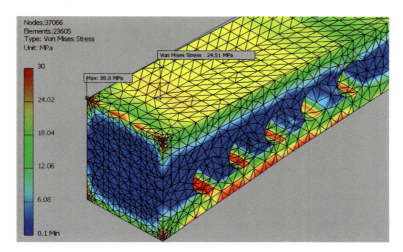

In the above example, stress singularities resulted from using automatic convergence, whereas the image below of the same model is showing very little change in stress in the area of interest by using the default mesh and no automatic convergence. Therefore, interpret results with care.

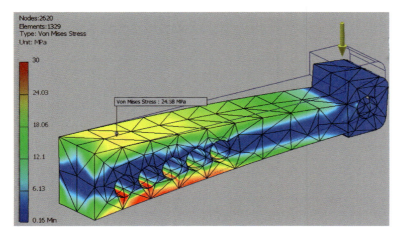

🔦 Gain further confidence in your results by using manual convergence, mentioned later in this chapter, when models have stress singularities present.

CHAPTER 1
The Stress Analysis Environment

Finally, another cause of stress singularity *is over-simplification of components*. Let's look at the following example.

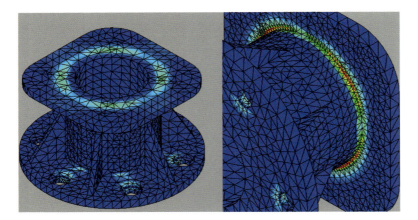

In this example, the fillets have been removed to simplify the analysis; however, when using automatic convergence, the maximum stress value does not converge as all the stress is concentrated around the edge, as shown. In this scenario it would advisable to unsuppress the fillets (or, in cases when fillets are not modeled, use fillets to distribute loads).

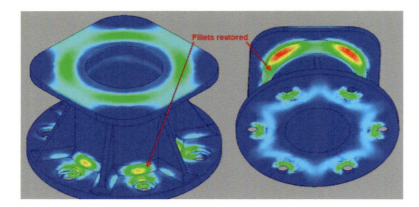

So, in brief to avoid stress singularities within models is to:

1. Avoid applying loads on points and small edges.
2. Avoid restraining faces with sharp corners, including points and small edges.
3. Apply fillets and chamfers to evenly distribute loads.

💡 Use linear elements when a model has stress singularities present, as they can capture stress singularities much better than the curve elements.

In some cases it is impossible to remove stress singularities, in which case careful interpretation of results is very important. One approach to this is detailed in Chapter 6.

Modal Analysis- an overview

Modal analysis determines modes to better understand the behaviour of components and structures under free vibration. Geometry, mass and constraints are the only factors that can affect modal analysis. Modes are inherent properties of a structure, and are determined by the material properties and boundary conditions of the structure. Each mode is defined by a natural frequency and a mode shape. Frequency is defined as cycles/s; for example 10 cycles/s is equivalent to 10 Hz. It is these frequencies that cause vibrations in components/structures. Most, if not all, engineered products cause vibration in today's for example the vibration felt through the steering wheel of a tyre caused by unbalanced tyres; the vibration felt through the floor when a passenger train goes past; and noise in airplanes especially at take-off, caused by revving of the aero-engines. By analyzing these modal shapes and frequencies, one can try to minimise these vibrations as they can cause failure in products by weakening the components and structures-due to fatigue. Another cause of failure due to vibrations is resonance -this is where two components have the same natural frequencies, resulting in excessive vibration and ultimately leading to destruction. Following are some examples of structures that have been affected by resonance and in some cases, leading to destruction or excessive vibration.

The Tacoma Bridge in Washington, USA, is a famous example of bridge failure due to resonance induced by wind. The bridge was completely reconstructed to better withstand variations in the wind speed etc. and with better damping to minimise and isolate vibrations in the bridge.

The Millennium Bridge in London, UK, was another example, in which lateral vibration was caused in the bridge as pedestrians walked over it. The greater the number of people walking on the bridge, the greater was the lateral movement. The bridge was closed soon after it was opened and remained closed for two further years. The problem was rectified by using a damping solution to absorb the movements, as stiffening the structure would have meant considerably altering the bridge.

Washing machines, which are used in many households, today can lead to excessive vibration of the drum induced by the full cycle spinning speed, and in some cases in combination with load weight of the wash. This in some extreme cases can lead the door to open, or even the machine to move from its original position, particularly in older machines.

CHAPTER 1
The Stress Analysis Environment

Helicopter Design is another field where vibration and resonance are critical issues. For example, if any of the components of a helicopter have frequencies that are close to the rotational speed of the rotors, then resonance of a component could occur, leading, for example, to a possible fatigue failure.

Thus, modal analysis is instrumental in helping us to better understand the structural flexibility and potential vibratory issues related to noise, fatigue, and resonance failures.

Natural frequencies – Basic theory

Theory for vibrations of continuous beams can be found in standard engineering textbooks. The natural frequencies of a simple cantilever can be determined theoretically using the following equation:

$$\frac{K^2}{2\pi}\sqrt{\frac{EI}{\rho AL^4}}$$

Where the K values for the first four modes are
1 – 1.8751
2 – 4.6941
3 – 7.8547
4 – 10.9955

And
E – Young's Modulus
I – Area moment of inertia
ρ – Density
A – Area
L – Length

For a simple plate, 30mm x 10mm x 300mm, made out of nylon 66, the first two calculated natural frequencies are 5.75Hz and 36.04Hz.

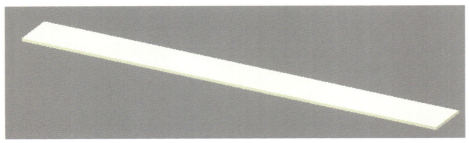

SECTION 1 -Stress Analysis Essentials

The following is a summary of results

	Theoretical	Modal analysis (mesh size 0.1)	Modal analysis (mesh size 0.05)	Modal analysis (mesh size 0.025)
Mode 1	5.75 Hz	6.33 Hz	5.9 Hz	5.85 Hz
Mode 2	36.04 Hz	43.87 Hz	37.09 Hz	36.67 Hz

Note: Mesh size refers to average element size

The followings settings were also used

1. Enhanced accuracy
2. Curved elements

For modal analysis, the mesh size can have impact on the accuracy of the results. An average element mesh size of 0.025 produces results within 2% when compared with theoretical results.

Preloaded modes

In some situations, however, the loads will affect the natural frequencies. An example would be a guitar string: as tension is applied, the frequency changes. Loads that produce membrane stresses will affect the natural frequency of the object. Tensile member stresses will increase the natural frequencies and compressive membrane stresses will lower them, whereas pure bending stress will not affect natural frequency.

Suspension bridge designs are classical examples of where extensive use is made of tensile members (cables) suspended via towers to hold up the road deck. The weight is held by the cables via the towers, which in turn transfer the weight to the ground. Tension within cables also provides rigidity to the structural integrity of the bridge.

Let's look at a simple tie rod example in which the tie rod is not prestressed; the first mode and shape of the rod are shown below, giving a natural frequency of 32.63 Hz.

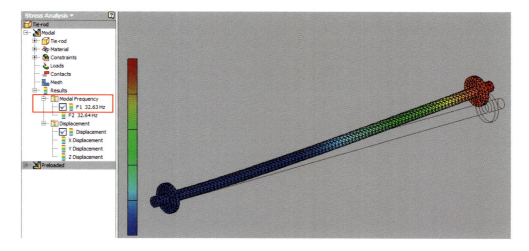

On the other hand, if a tensile load of 1000 N is applied to prestress the tie rod, the natural frequency of the first mode almost doubles to 60.20 Hz.

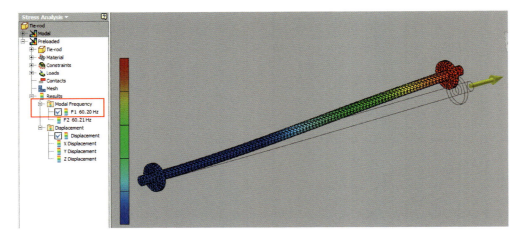

As we have now covered the basics of stress and modal theory, we will now go over the user interface of Autodesk Inventor Simulation.

Stress Analysis Workflow

The process of creating a dynamic simulation study involves four core steps:

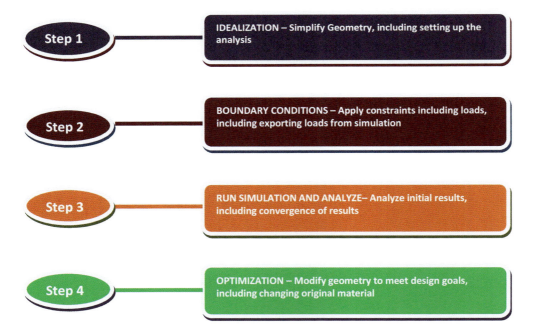

Step 1 — IDEALIZATION – Simplify Geometry, including setting up the analysis

Step 2 — BOUNDARY CONDITIONS – Apply constraints including loads, including exporting loads from simulation

Step 3 — RUN SIMULATION AND ANALYZE– Analyze initial results, including convergence of results

Step 4 — OPTIMIZATION – Modify geometry to meet design goals, including changing original material

Stress Analysis User Interface

Stress Analysis can be accessed from both the Part and Assembly environment via the Analysis tab.

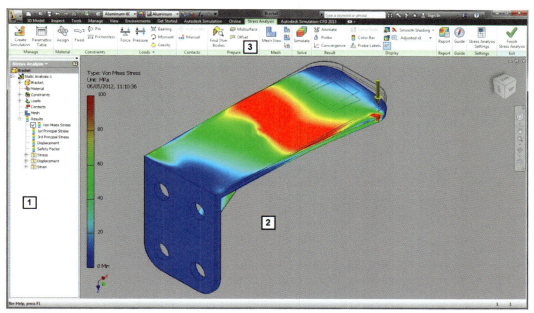

1. Stress Analysis browser
2. Stress Analysis graphic window
3. Stress Analysis panel

Stress analysis browser

Displays the simulations with part or assembly and simulation parameters in a hierarchical view with nested levels of feature and attribute information. You can:

1. Copy whole simulations or simulation objects between simulations
   1. Right click on a node for context menu options
2. Expand the folders, select the nodes, and see the selection cross-highlighted in the graphic region.

Stress analysis graphic window

Display's the model geometry and simulation results. Updates to show the current status of the simulation including applying boundary conditions and loads with the help of view manipulation tools

Stress analysis panel

Stress Analysis tab	Workflow stage	Description
Create Simulation / Parametric Table — Manage	Step 1	**Create Simulation** – Here you decide whether you need to create a stress, modal, or a parametric analysis.
	Step 4	**Parametric Table** – Define design constraints including mass, stress, deformation, etc.
Assign — Material	Step 2	**Material** – Create and apply material for the components if not already defined in the Part environment.
Fixed / Pin / Frictionless — Constraints		**Constraints** – Represent how a part is fixed or attached to other parts in reality, and thus restricting their motion.
Force / Pressure / Bearing / Moment / Gravity — Loads		**Loads** - Represent the external forces that are exerted on a component. During normal use, the component is expected to withstand these loads and continue to perform as intended.
Automatic / Manual — Contacts		**Contacts** – Create contacts between components automatically or manually. There are seven types of contacts including bonded.
Find Thin Bodies / Midsurface / Offset — Prepare		**Prepare** – Tools to create surfaces specifically for thin parts. Find Thin Bodies command automatically detects components suitable for midsurface creation
Mesh View — Mesh		**Mesh** – Preview and create mesh, including global and local mesh refinement.
Simulate — Solve	Step 3	**Solve** – Run the simulation to analyze the results as a consequence of defining materials, constraints and loads.
Animate / Probe / Convergence — Result		**Results** – View the stress and deformation results to provide an informed decision on whether the component will function under the defined loads and constraints.
Actual — Display		**Display** – Modify color plots, including displaying max and min values.

Stress analysis panel continued

Stress Analysis tab	Optional Workflows	Description
Report	-	**Report** – Generate an html report of the results to share.
Guide		**Guide** – Provides guidance, when activated, on how to best set up and run an analysis.
Stress Analysis Settings	-	**Settings** – Can predefine initial settings, including contact tolerance and mesh settings.

Manage tab

This is the first step in creating a stress analysis study.

Create Simulation

Here you can define whether you want to carry out single static analysis, modal analysis or a parametric study, including the option of selecting different levels of detail.

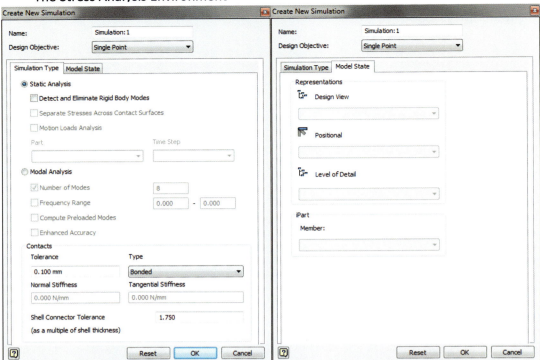

Design Objective – Here you define whether you want to carry out a single or parametric optimization; this is discussed in the next section.

Simulation Type - Here you define whether a stress or modal analysis is to be carried out.

Model State – For an assembly, you can choose any **Design View** and **Level of Detail** on which to perform analysis.

 Use **Level of Detail** (with all parts suppressed, except one) when there is a need to analyze a component, which has loads exported from Simulation.

Static Analysis

There are three settings when performing stress analysis.

Detect and Eliminate Rigid Body Modes - It is possible that a model may not have enough structural constraints to fix it completely in space. For example, imagine a cube the top face of which is loaded with normal pressure, and the bottom face of which is constrained by a frictionless constraint. One frictionless constraint is not enough to uniquely define the position of the cube; it can slide sideways as a whole, and we call such movement a rigid body mode. For such cases of incomplete constraints we have a special algorithm that eliminates rigid body movements from the displacements, if **Detect and Eliminate Rigid Body Modes** is selected. The cube as illustrated below will compress and expand sideways, but its center of mass will stay in place.

 Select **Detect and Eliminate Rigid Body Modes** if you intend to use frictionless constraints only.

If rigid body motion is detected in an assembly analysis, this option will automatically be switched on if it was not initially selected.

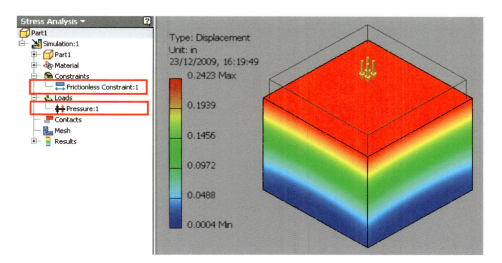

Separate Stresses Across Contact Surfaces - If two bodies have the same material and are connected by the bonded contact, theoretically both displacements and stresses should be continuous across the boundary. In FEA solution, because the meshes on the bodies do not exactly match, we may end up with different stresses on different sides of the boundary. By default, we compute average of the two sides and show it as the stress at both sides of the boundary. However, when elements on one side are substantially smaller than on the other, and the distribution of the stress on the contact is important, the user can turn the **Separate Stresses Across Contact Surfaces** option on, and have each side's stress computed, resulting in differing stress plots on adjacent contact faces.

 This option only applies to bonded contacts and same materials.

Motion Loads Analysis – This option will only be available if the part to be analyzed has its loads transferred from the dynamic simulation study. If multiple time steps have been transferred then the user can select the specific time to be used for the stress analysis.

 You can copy and edit the first simulation and select another time step to compare the results with the first. When copying, all the boundary conditions including the mesh and loads will also be copied.

Modal Analysis

When performing modal analysis there are four settings which can be defined.

Number of modes – Here you define how many modes you want the software to calculate. You can specify any value between 1 and 200, with 8 being the default value. The following shows one mode, as one mode was chosen.

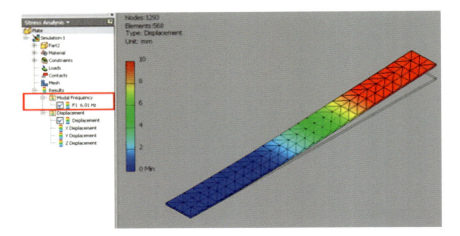

Frequency Range – Here you can specify the natural frequency range you want the software to calculate. If you have not constrained your model then you can specify a higher value than zero for your initial value as this will not calculate the first six modes, which will be zero due to rigid body motion reflecting the six degrees of freedom, with no distortion of the body shape.

Compute Preloaded Modes – Select to compute stress on the model and then compute modes for the pre-stressed condition. The following example illustrates that natural frequency increases from 6.01 to 105.52Hz as a result of applying a tensile force of 1000N.

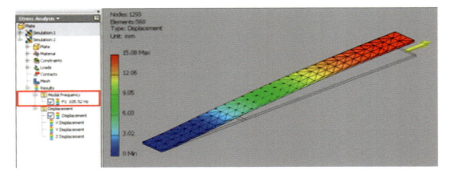

You cannot run a preload modal analysis if you apply a compressive or bending load within Autodesk Inventor Simulation.

Enhanced Accuracy – This option, if selected, increases the accuracy of the calculated frequency values by an order of magnitude (10). The following example illustrates that the frequency is very similar at 104.7 Hz less (than 1% difference); the result can be assumed to be converged.

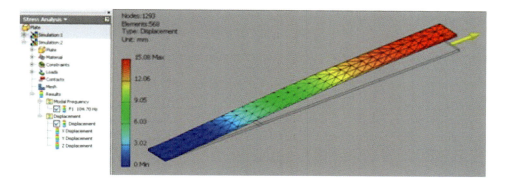

Contacts

If an assembly is being analyzed then you can also define a contact tolerance setting and type of contact to be automatically created.

Tolerance

For solid element mesh a tolerance of 0.1mm will create contacts between all components that have gaps of less than or equal to 0.1mm.

 This setting applies to component faces that have been used to create mid-surfaces (for thin elements) and not the actual mid-surfaces created.

Shell Connector Tolerance

For thin elements a tolerance of 1.750 will create connectors between surfaces that make up the part that have gaps of less than or equal to 1.750 x shell thickness.

Let's take the following example, which has a plate thickness of 0.5mm and a radii of 2mm.

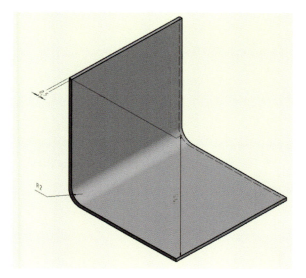

CHAPTER 1
The Stress Analysis Environment

Using the default setting if we select the mid-surface command, in the prepare tab, we get the following mid-surfaces created, for a single component as shown.

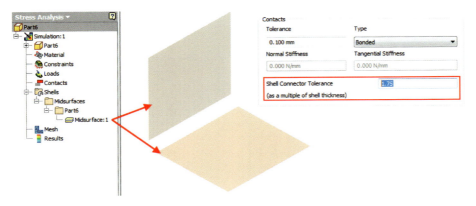

The above image shows only one mid-surface created although it seems like two surfaces. This is a result of having a fillet which develops a variable thickness which cannot be converted to a mid-surface. As it stands these surfaces are not connected and the contact tolerance only works for assemblies. This new shell connector tolerance applies to only parts and creates connectors to link mid-surfaces with gaps.

The default Shell Connector Tolerance of 0.875mm (1.750x0.5) is to small as the gap between the two closest edges is approx 2.475mm (shortest distance). In order to create connectors we need to increase the shell connector tolerance to at least 5 which will give a tolerance of 2.5mm. Doing this will create connectors as shown

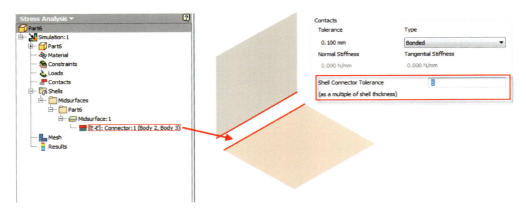

 The shell connector tolerance only connects surfaces at its edges and not surfaces. Therefore this connector will not work for I-Beam type connections.

 If possible simplify components by removing fillets/chamfers to avoid creating gaps between surfaces for single components.

Parametric Table

One of the unique and powerful features of Inventor Simulation is the ability to perform parametric optimization studies

Design constraints including mass and others can be accessed and selected by right clicking in the **Design Constraints** row.

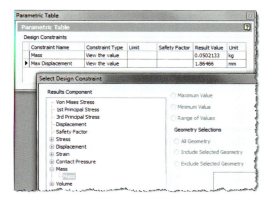

The **Constraint Type** values can be set to any of the following:

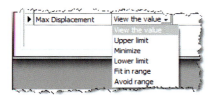

For example, if the criteria are to minimize the mass, we would select **Minimize** and then the optimum design configuration would be selected automatically.

By right clicking on any component within the browser, we can select **Show Parameters** and then choose any parameters we need to optimize.

Once the parameters have been selected, the parameter range can be produced by either of the following two methods:

1. If specific values are required, specify the value separated by commas, as illustrated below:

> 1,4,6,13   will produce the specified individual values

2. If you are generally interested in seeing the effect of a parameter, the parameter range can be produced as illustrated below:

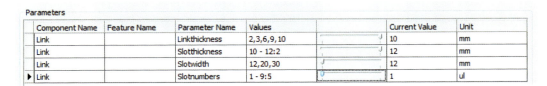

$1 - 9 : 5$ will produce three more values equally spaced between 1 and 9; that is 3,5,7

Parameters

Component Name	Feature Name	Parameter Name	Values		Current Value	Unit
Link		Linkthickness	2,3,6,9,10		10	mm
Link		Slotthickness	10 - 12:2		12	mm
Link		Slotwidth	12,20,30		12	mm
▶ Link		Slotnumbers	1 - 9:5		1	ul

Once the design constraints and parameters are defined, the parameter configurations can be produced by right clicking anywhere in the parameter rows and selecting any of the following:

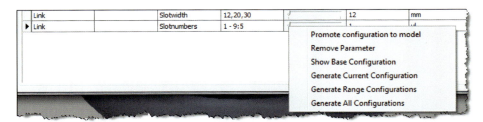

Promote configuration to model – Promotes the value to the part parameter table, over riding the original value.

Remove Parameter - Removes the parameter from the parametric table and updates the geometry with the parameter base value.

Show Base Configuration - Displays the base configuration of the model in the graphics region.

Generate Single Configuration – Generates and displays the current value, if not already selected.

Generate Range Configurations - Generates a configuration for each value in the specified range for that parameter row.

 Select **Generate Range Configurations** for each range individually rather than generate all.

Generate All Configurations - Creates configurations for all the values in the parametric table.

 Selecting **Generate All Configurations** can take a very long time, especially if there is a large number of parameters.

Simulate this configuration – Simulates the selected configuration only.

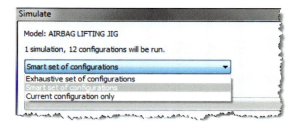

Simulate this configuration – Simulates the selected configuration only.

Exhaustive set of configurations – Simulates all the configurations and can take a very long time.

Smart set of configurations – The software will determine and simulate the optimum number of configurations, not necessarily all.

Material tab

Normally, most components will have their materials assigned within the Part environment, thus removing the need to assign materials, as they will come across directly from the Part environment.

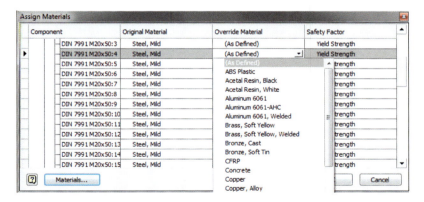

However, the materials can be overridden by selecting other materials from the materials library. New materials can also be created via the **Materials** button.

Further, the safety factor can be calculated from either the **Yield Strength** or **Ultimate Strength** values.

 Factor of safety is normally calculated based on Yield Strength.

 Safety Factor values below zero will not produce valid stress results.

Constraints tab

Fixed constraint

The location can be defined by specifying either a point, an edge or a face. A fixed constraint allows you to restrict the translational direction of the component in the x, y, z direction. For example, if a component is fixed or bonded, you will normally fix all three directions.

Pin constraint

The location can only be defined by a cylindrical face and this constraint is typically used where holes are supported by bearings or pins. Typically, for a bearing or pin, you free the tangential direction to enable the surface to rotate freely.

 A pin constraint is the same as a fixed constraint if the tangential direction is also fixed.

Frictionless Constraint

The location can only be defined by a planar face and enables a component to freely slide along a plane and prevent motion normal to the sliding plane or surface.

 Frictional constraints can also be used to model symmetry boundary conditions, for example a quarter or half model.

Loads tab

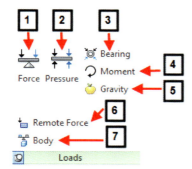

1. Force
2. Pressure
3. Bearing Loads
4. Moment
5. Gravity
6. Remote Loads
7. Body Load

These loads can be generally categorized into

- General loads
- Face loads
- Body loads

General loads

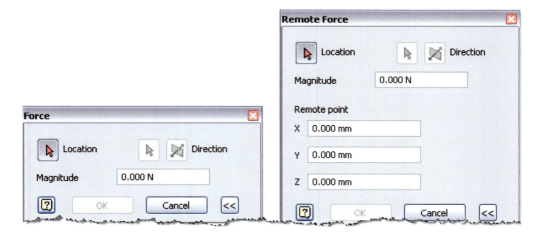

To fully define general loads, a location, direction, and magnitude are all required. Location can be defined by planar face and, in the case of force, can also be defined by an edge or point. Direction can be defined by either a planar face, work plane, edge or work axis.

Do not apply force on holes as this will not simulate reality. This is because the force will be applied on the complete whole whereas, in reality, the force is only applied on a portion of the hole via, for example, a pin.

Face loads

With the exception of pressure, to fully define other face loads, a location, direction, and magnitude are all required. Location can only be defined by a planar face for pressure and moment and, in the case of bearing load, the face needs to be cylindrical. With the exception of pressure, direction can be defined by a planar face, work plane, an edge or work axis. The direction of the pressure is always normal to the face.

 Always use bearing loads to specify force in holes

 Pressure is related to area, so, if a component is being parametrically optimized, take care as pressure can also change if the area changes.

Body loads

To fully define body loads, a direction and a magnitude are required. Direction can be defined by either a planar face, work plane, edge or work axis.

For all loads, magnitude can be specified by entering an absolute value or a mathematical expression. An example of a mathematical expression could be 100 x sin (45 deg).

With the exception of pressure, the direction and magnitude can alternatively be specified by using vector components

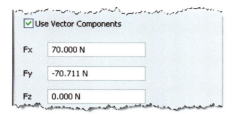

With the exception of body loads and gravity, the display glyph color and scale can be altered in addition to the name.

 When applying loads, it is advisable not to apply loads at points or small edges as this can produce very high localized stresses.

Contacts tab

There are seven types of contacts in Inventor Simulation Suite.

Types of contacts

1. **Bonded** – Bonds contact faces to each other, for example, in fabricated structures.

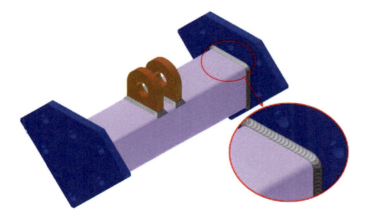

SECTION 1 -Stress Analysis Essentials

2.   **Separation** – Allows adjacent contact faces to separate and slide under deformation; for example, loose bolt hole connections.

3.   **Sliding/No Separation** – Maintains contact between adjacent faces and allows sliding when under deformation; for example, tight bolt hole connections.

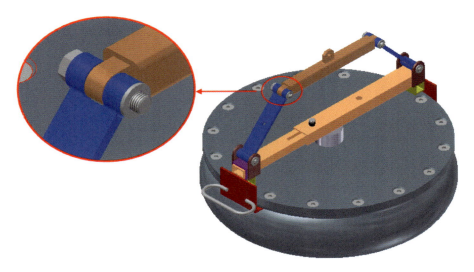

4.   **Separation / No Sliding** – Separates contact faces partially or fully without sliding.

5.   **Shrink Fit / Sliding** – Similar to **Separation** contact, with the addition of allowing for initial overlaps between components, creating prestress conditions.

6.   **Shrink Fit/No Sliding** - Similar to **Separation/No sliding** contact, with the addition of allowing for initial overlaps between components, creating prestress conditions; for example, in seal and pipe/clamp connections.

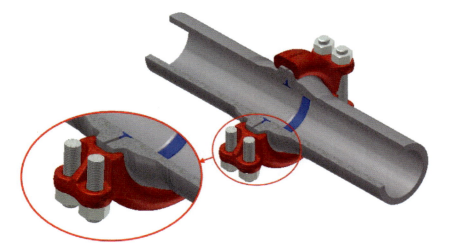

7.   **Spring** - Creates spring conditions between two components by applying stiffness properties.

The process of creating contacts

There are two ways to create contacts: automatically and manually. The automatic method is by far the quickest and creates contacts between adjacent faces within the predefined settings, as below.

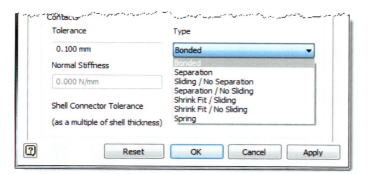

In some cases, the automatic method of creating contacts will not detect adjacent faces that have a higher gap than the predefined contact tolerance settings. In this scenario, you can use the manual method of creating contacts to create a contact.

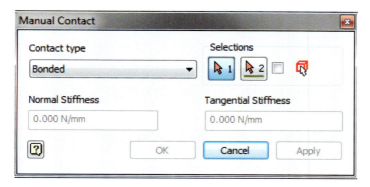

Prepare tab

Find Thin Bodies

This tool when selected will automatically determine components to be converted to surfaces, using the mid-surface option.

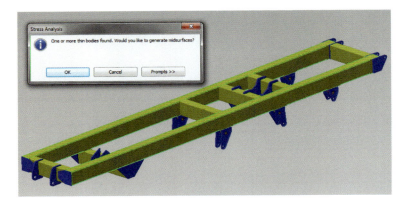

Generally components with a cross section to length ratio greater than 1:250 will be automatically selected as shown below

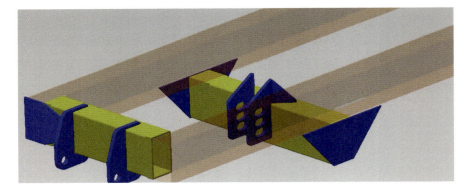

The actual ratio value is calculated using the equation below

Given that:
vol = volume of a body
area = surface area of the body

ratio = $(36 \times \pi \times vol^2)/(area^3)^{1/6}$

If a ratio is over 250 a warning dialogue will appear indicating that the component should be meshed using thin elements.

 Find Thin Bodies tool can only be used once. To create extra surfaces use the **Midsurface** and **Offset** mentioned next

Midsurface

This command is used to select any component for a which a mid-surface is required that was not automatically detected using the **Find Thin Bodies** tool.

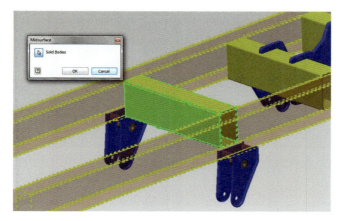

 Selecting any face on the component will automatically select all faces of the component to be converted to a midsurface.

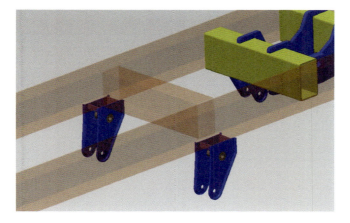

 Creating midsurfaces will create gaps between components (surfaces), so take care in manipulating results as in reality there will be no gaps. See Example 1 - Thin Elements

 If components are made from the same material then I suggest creating a shrinkwrap before creating a midsurface.

Offset

This command unlike the midsurface gives the user control on what feature/face of the component is to be used to create a midsurface by unselecting **Automatic Face Chain** and specifying the thickness of the component, as illustrated below.

 This can be ideally used to simplify the components for the purposes of analysis and meshing, as an alternative to exclude from simulation.

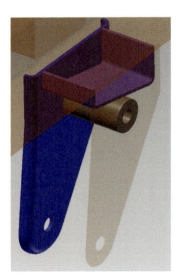

 Use this command if you have split faces as this command will not merge the surfaces into one.

Example 1 – Thin Elements

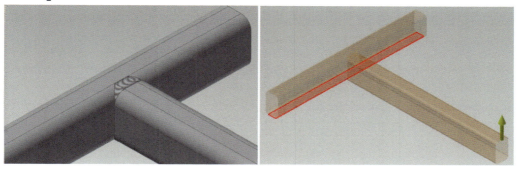

Here I am going to illustrate the difference in results, specifically in the area where the box section are connected, when treating each member of fabrication individually and as a single component. The key feature to note is the radii of the box sections which if removed can result in providing extra stiffness in the model, thus can produce inaccurate results. The box section is fixed at the bottom face and a load of 20N is applied on the edge of the other box section as shown above

Lets first have a look at the results of the model with each box section as a separate components. The first thing you will note is the gap as a result of creating midsurfaces for each box section as shown below

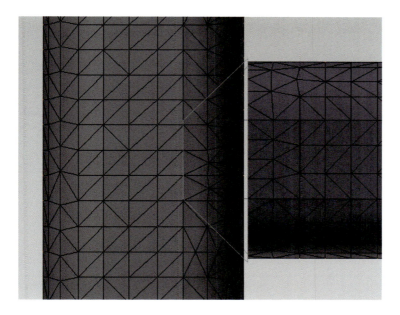

CHAPTER 1

The Stress Analysis Environment

We now look at the YY Stresses in the box sections and note the highest stresses are at the connection point as expected.

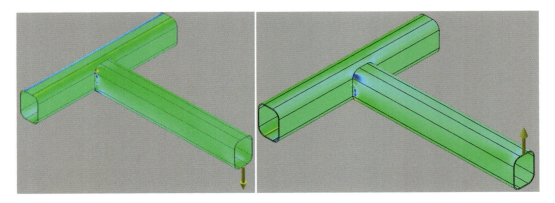

Now looking at the results for the shrinkwrap we can see that results are more accurately represented around the weld area as illustrated below.

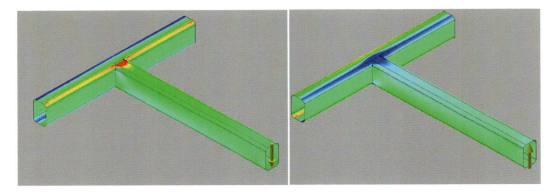

So take care when analyzing results in the areas of the gaps created as a result of using thin elements.

TRY IT! – **Open boxsection.*iam***

Mesh tab

Mesh View

Mesh

1. Generate and Preview Mesh
2. Mesh Setting
3. Local Mesh Control
4. Convergence Settings

These tools can be further categorized into the following:

1. Manual mesh refinement
2. Automatic mesh refinement (or automatic convergence)

Manual mesh refinement

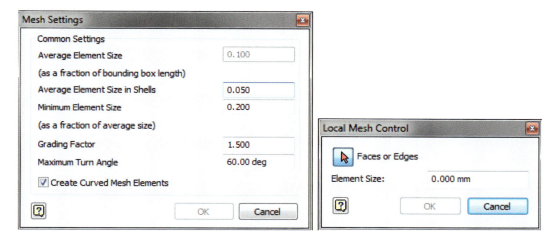

In this edition of the book there are two average element size values that can be specified one for solid elements and the other for shell elements. This gives the ability to have different sizes for models that have both solid and thin elements. They both operate the same way and thus only solid elements are used in the following sections to explain average element size and other setting.

Here, an example will be used to explain the manual mesh refinement tools.

Example 2 – Mesh Settings

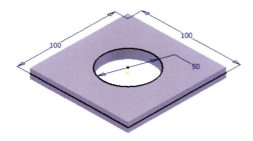

Where the thickness of the component is 10 mm

Average Element Size – Initially, we will check the effect of altering the **Average Element Size**.

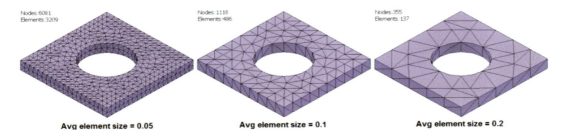

| Avg element size = 0.05 | Avg element size = 0.1 | Avg element size = 0.2 |

Using a smaller number will produce a denser mesh, as illustrated above.

 As a guide, to determine the size of an element, the following can be used:

$$Size\ of\ mesh\ element\ =\ Longest\ parameter\ of\ object\ \ x\ Average\ element\ size$$

So, for an average element size of 0.2, the mesh size, for example, would be approximately

$$Size\ of\ mesh\ element\ =\ 100\ x\ 0.2 = 20$$

The maximum **Average Element Size** that can be specified is 1.

A denser mesh will take a longer time to analyze.

Minimum Element Size - Is a highly sensitive parameter and, as a rule of thumb, can remain unaltered at a value of 0.2. If the value needs changing, use any number in the following range:

$$0.2 \geq minimum\ element\ size\ \geq 0.5$$

Grading Factor - Specifies the maximum ratio of adjacent mesh edges for transitioning between coarse and fine regions. A smaller grading factor produces a more uniform mesh.

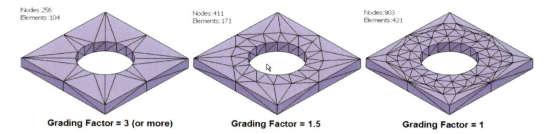

Nodes:256
Elements:104

Nodes:411
Elements:171

Nodes:903
Elements:421

Grading Factor = 3 (or more)   Grading Factor = 1.5   Grading Factor = 1

Using a smaller number will produce a denser mesh, as illustrated above.

 The value for the grading factor can be specified between 1 and 10. The recommended range is:

$$1.5 \geq Grading\ Factor \leq 3$$

Maximum Turn Angle - Allows you to control the number of elements along a 90° arc. Specifying 60° will at least create two or more elements to fill a 90° arc, whereas a maximum turn angle of 30° will create at least three or more elements to fill a 90° arc.

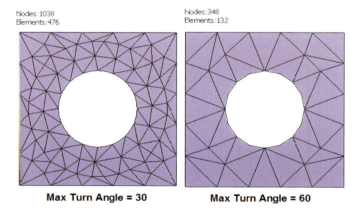

Nodes:1038
Elements:476

Nodes:348
Elements:132

Max Turn Angle = 30   Max Turn Angle = 60

A small angle value of 15, for example, can produce a very dense mesh, especially when the model contains holes and radii. The recommended range is:

$$30 \geq Max\ Turn\ Angle \leq 60$$

It is advisable to suppress small features to avoid creating significantly more elements

Create Curved Mesh Elements - Represent models with circular features more accurately than straight elements.

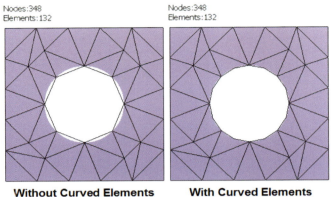

Without Curved Elements   **With Curved Elements**

 Curved elements may help to produce more accurate results.

Local Mesh Control – Is used to further refine the model by specifying an absolute value on faces or edges.

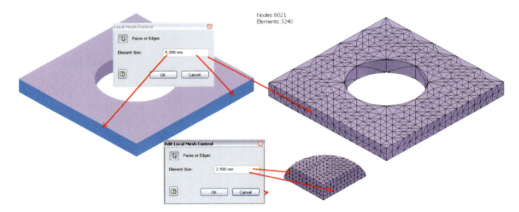

Specifying a value of 5mm will create two elements vertically on the side faces, as the height of the base is 10mm. A local mesh size of 2.5mm will create four elements vertically on the selected side faces.

TRY IT! – Open plate.*ipt*

Automatic mesh refinement (or automatic convergence)

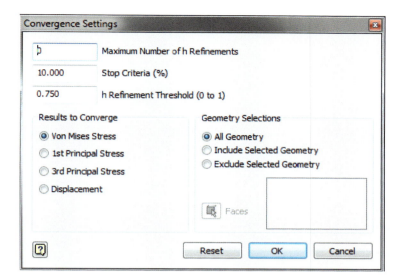

Maximum Number of h Refinements – Here, you specify the maximum number of mesh refinements based around maximum stresses. Values higher than 5, may result in stress singularities, and take a long time to analyze.

Stop Criteria (%) – Is used for convergence between two consecutive refinements. If the difference between the two refinements is less than 10%, the convergence process will stop.

H Refinement Threshold (0 to 1) – A value of 0 will include all elements in the model as candidates for refinement, whereas a value 1 will exclude all elements from the H-refinement process. The default value is 0.75, which means that the top 25% elements around the high stress area will likely be candidates for refinement.

 Use **Exclude Selected Geometry** where models have stress singularities.

 Use a lower value if the model has multiple stress singularity areas.

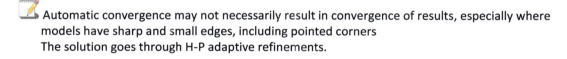 Automatic convergence may not necessarily result in convergence of results, especially where models have sharp and small edges, including pointed corners
The solution goes through H-P adaptive refinements.

Here, again another example will be used to explain the convergence settings required to automatically refine the mesh and convergence of results.

CHAPTER 1
The Stress Analysis Environment

Example 3 – Convergence Settings

In this example we need to determine whether the component can withstand a load of 1000N, which is fixed at each of the bolt holes. Secondly, we need to determine the maximum stress, which is required, for example, to determine fatigue life.

Using a mesh setting of **Average Element Size** of 0.05, the example is analyzed with peak stresses around all the bolt holes and fillets. The convergence plot shows that the results have not converge with the initial P-refinement (with H -refinement set to 0).

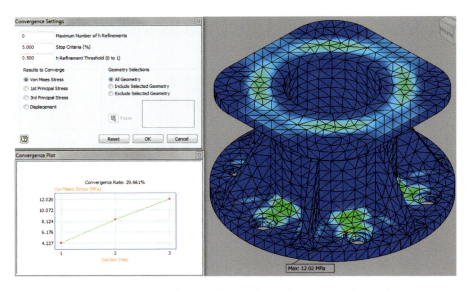

To obtain convergence we will rerun the analysis, this time with **Maximum Number of h Refinements** set to 2 and the **Stop criteria (%)** set to 10. The H-refinement threshold will be reduced to 0.5, as we have multiple areas of high stress. This value will refine at least 50% of the model mesh around peak stress regions.

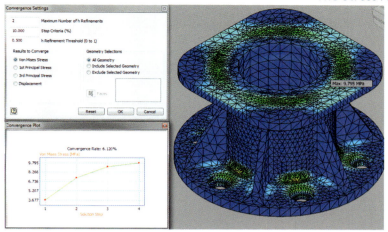

From the results we can see that the stress have converged at the first iteration of H-P Refinement Process (point 4) and therefore does not need to go to second iteration of H-P Refinement Process (point 5). Further, it is important to note that the mesh has been refined around the bolt holes, and other areas of the model, where there was high stress.

In cases where the model has stress singularities, you can still use automatic convergence with **Excluded Selected Geometry** option selected to obtain automatic convergence of results in key areas of interest, as illustrated below.

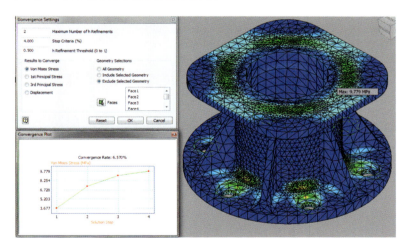

The mesh is not refined around areas of excluded geometry (the top faces of the bolt hole).

TRY IT! – Open *Coupling.ipt*

An alternative process to using the automatic convergence where models have stress singularities is to use manual convergence

Manual Convergence

1. Run analysis with **Average Element Size** of 0.1
2. Rerun analysis with **Average Element Size** of 0.05
3. Rerun analysis with **Average Element Size** 0.025

If the difference between the first and last analysis is within 10%, you can assume that your results have converged. Use the color bar to modify legend values to help visualize results better by isolating the stress singularity results.

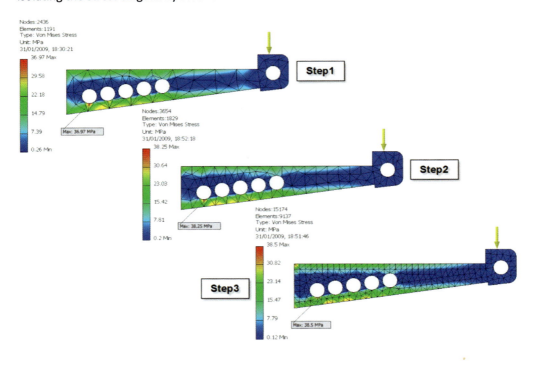

TRY IT! – Open *Snap-fit.ipt*

Results tab

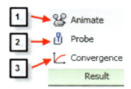

1. Animate
2. Probe
3. Convergence

Inventor Simulation now offers many more result displays, including planar (XX, YY, ZZ) and shear stresses (XY, XZ, YZ).

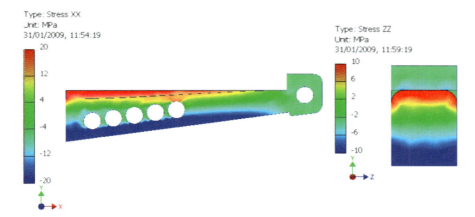

The complete list of result displays available is shown below.

Animate

Creates a video file of the animation

 For a smoother display, increase the number of steps.

 The valid range of steps is 3 ≤ **Steps** ≤ 30.

Probe

Probe helps to pinpoint the key areas of interest in the model, especially when the model has maximum results distorted, due to stress singularities.

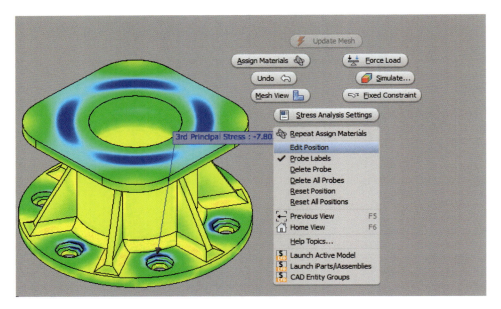

Convergence plot

This helps us to gain confidence by illustrating that the results in the area of interest have converged, as illustrated below.

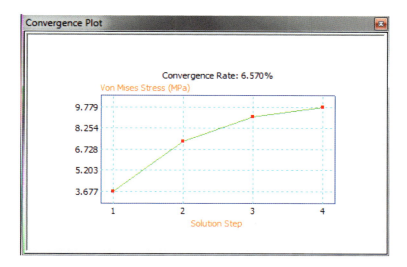

Every analysis goes through an automatic P-refinement. If the results have not converged, then H-refinement can be activated. The above example shows that the results have converged within four iterations - the first three being of P-refinement and the fourth being of H-refinement (for example, H-refinement set to 1). If the results do not converge then the H-refinement value can be further increased to 2, 3 or 4.

For parts, the first three convergence plot points are related to P-refinement.

For assemblies, the first two convergence plot points are related to P-refinement

Display tab

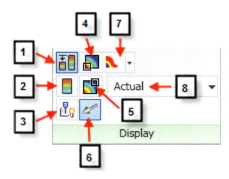

1. Apply Uniform Scale
2. Color Bar
3. Show Probe Labels
4. Show Maximum Value

5. Show Minimum Value
6. Show Boundary Conditions
7. Display Results
8. Adjust Displacement Scale

Apply uniform scale

This is switched off by default and can be useful when carrying out a parametric optimization study. When activated, the color bar scale remains the same when viewing different configurations and thus allows you to compare results visually.

 The color bar is scaled based on the maximum and minimum values within the parametric configuration results.

 Use **Apply Uniform Scale** when viewing a component when the rest of the assembly is excluded from the results.

Color Bar

The color bar is probably the most important tool within the Display panel and, when effectively used, can help you to understand the results with ease. It can be displayed in various locations in the graphic window using the **Position** setting. The **Maximum** and **Minimum** threshold values can be altered by unchecking the **Maximum** and **Minimum** values.

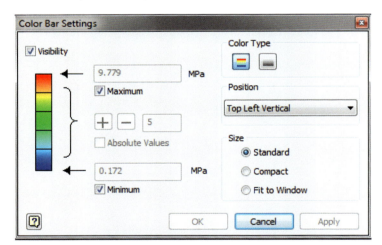

 The numbers of color legends can only be changed when **Contour Shading** is selected. **Smooth Shading** by default will use the maximum number of color legends.

 Alter **Maximum** and **Minimum** values to help isolate stress singularities.

Show probe labels

Displays all the probe labels created by the user

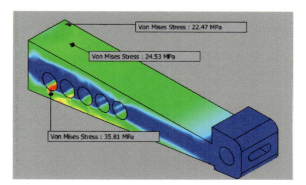

The position of the probe can be altered by right clicking its label and selecting **Edit Position**. This will help to identify whether the value has increased or decreased around the original selection area.

Individual probes can be deleted by right clicking the probe and selecting **Delete Probe**, or **Delete All Probes**.

Show Maximum and Minimum values

Displays the maximum and minimum values and their locations on the model as illustrated below

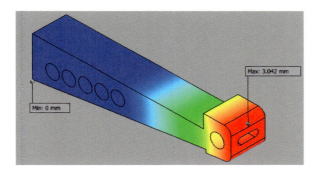

Show boundary conditions

Displays all the boundary conditions, including the loads applied on the model.

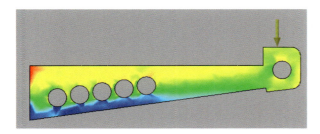

Display results

Here, you can decide whether you want **Smooth**, **Contour** and **No Shading** display.

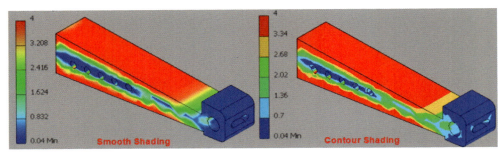

Adjust displacement display

You can adjust the scale of the results to obtain a better indication of whether boundary conditions applied are correct.

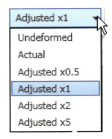

 Adjust the scale so that the deformation is visible before selecting **Animate results**, as animations without visible deformation can be less visual.

Report tab

Autodesk Inventor – in addition to standard html format – now lets you create reports in mhtml (single web page) and rich text formats (Microsoft Word documents), making it very easy to customize the reports to specific requirements.

Microsoft Word is required to generate the RTF file.

In addition to the ability to customize settings from the **General**, **Properties** and **Simulation** tabs from with the **Report Generator** dialogue box, there are now additional settings within the format tab:

Use Dynamic Content - Select to include size buttons for image width and buttons that you can click to collapse or expand the associated sections.

 Not available for the RTF format

Create OLE Link - Select to create an OLE link from the model browser to the report. The report icon displays under the Third Party folder in the model browser. To edit the report, double click the icon or right-click and select **Edit**.

 Not available for the HTML format

Stress Analysis Report

Autodesk®

Analyzed File:	Snap-fit-feA.ipt
Autodesk Inventor Version:	2011 Beta2 (Build 150194000, 194) Debug 0
Creation Date:	25/12/2009, 14:16
Simulation Author:	Wasim
Summary:	

Project Info (iProperties)

Summary

Author	Wasim Younis

Project

Part Number	Snap-fit-feA
Designer	WY
Cost	£0.00

Status

Design Status	WorkInProgress

Physical

Material	Nylon-6/6
Density	1.13 g/cm^3
Mass	0.00532516 kg
Area	2804.8 mm^2

Results

Result Summary

Name	Minimum	Maximum
Volume	4712.43 mm^3	
Mass	0.00532504 kg	
Von Mises Stress	0.0396384 MPa	4.84543 MPa
Displacement	0 mm	0.565338 mm
Safety Factor	15 ul	15 ul

Figures

Von Mises Stress

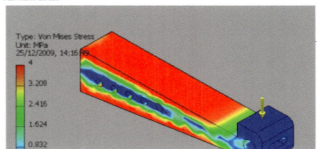

Guide tab

The Guide is a useful tool for novice and intermediate users who want advice on certain aspect of simulation. The Guide tool is accessible from the Analysis panel and by right-clicking Loads, Constraints, Contacts and Results guide.

Below is an example: the Constraints Guide

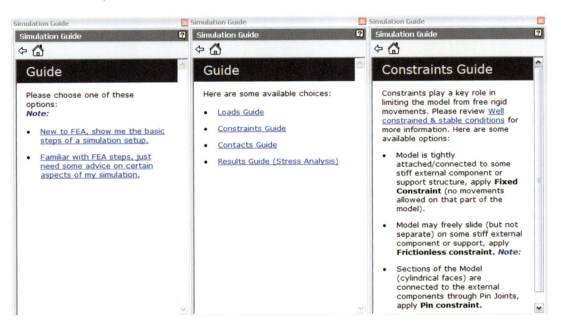

Settings tab

Stress Analysis
Settings

Settings

Allows you to predefine settings for current and preceding analyses.

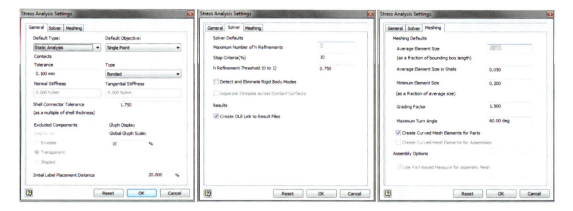

Refer to the specific sections for a detailed explanation of the individual settings.

Section 2 -
STRESS ANALYSIS
Design Problems
using SOLID ELEMENTS

DP1 – Cyclic Symmetry Analysis

Design of Industrial Centrifugal Fan Blades
(Design Problem Courtesy of Halifax Fan Ltd)

Key features and workflows introduced in this design problem

	Key Features/Workflows
1	Cyclic symmetry
2	Manual convergence of results

Introduction

Halifax Fan Ltd is one of the world's foremost manufacturers of industrial fans. They design and manufacture a full range of centrifugal fans from a wide range of materials, including mild and stainless steel, from their manufacturing operations in the UK and China. They supply a wide range of industrial customers, including power, pharmaceutical, chemical, nuclear, and marine markets all over the world.

Halifax Fan is fully BSI certified to BS EN ISO9001 – 2000 and manufactures fans to many industrial standards including API 673, API 560, Shell DEP, and ATEX. Many of these designs are engineered to meet the customer's exact requirements and, thus, the company offers a wide range of services on and off site, including stress relief laser shaft alignment, site performance testing, vibration analysis, consultation, problem solving, repairs, and energy testing. As a consequence of offering special bespoke solutions, Halifax is regularly asked by its customers to validate their designs prior to delivery.

Some of the typical requirements include determining the following:
- The maximum stress and deflection of the fan blade.
- The factor of safety of the new design.

In addition to the above requirements, the design criteria to be used for this design problem are as follows;
- Material to be used is either mild Steel or high strength low alloy *
- Factor of Safety required is 1.5
- Maximum deflection to be less than 0.5mm.
- Maximum blade thickness not to exceed 5mm.

* Halifax Fan actually use Carbon Steel to BS EN 10025 grade S275JR for their fans

Workflow of Design Problem 1

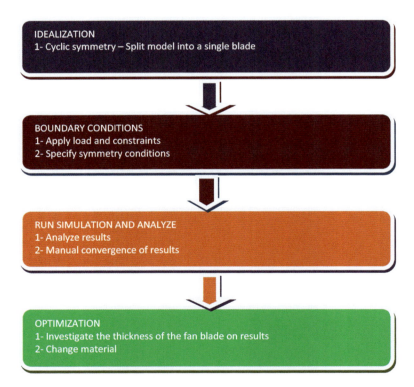

Idealization

Halifax Fans can range from simple small fans to large detailed fans. In the cases of large detailed fans, the size of the mesh can become very large and the time taken to analyze the results can become very lengthy.

Most fans comprise a number of similar blades and, when in operation, the deflection and stress induced in the blades are identical and for this reason it is only necessary to analyze one blade of the fan. This simplification approach is also referred to as cyclic symmetry and it's significantly reduces the model size, giving more scope to refine and analyze the results efficiently. Therefore, in the following steps, the fan model is split such that only one blade remains.

Cyclic symmetry – Split model into a single blade

1. Open *Fan*.ipt

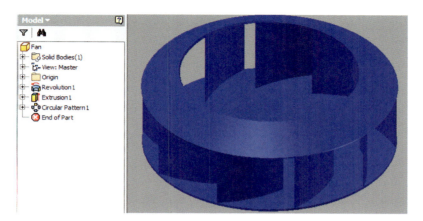

2. Create a new sketch on the YZ plane to the following dimensions

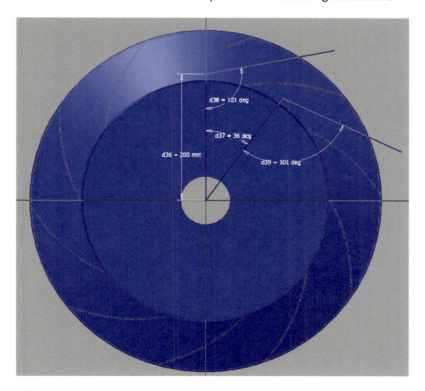

💡 It will help to change Visual Style to Wireframe or Shaded with Hidden Edges when creating the sketch, as this will allow you to see blades under the top plate.

 Make all 4 lines equal to 200mm.

DP1 – Cyclic Symmetry Analysis

As there are 10 blades, we need to the split the model by 36° angles.

$$\text{Angle of Split to create single blade } = \frac{360}{\text{Number of Blades}} = \frac{360}{10} = 36°$$

3. Select **Finish Sketch** > Select **Shaded** for **Visual Style**

4. Using the **Split** feature, split the part using the sketch created

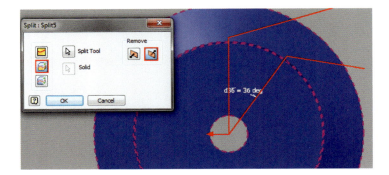

5. Click **OK**.

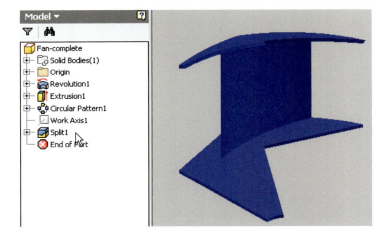

Now, in the next section, the boundary conditions will be applied to the single fan blade.

Boundary conditions

6. Select **Environments** tab > Select **Stress Analysis**

Apply load and constraints

7.   Select **Create Simulation** > Specify **Single-Blade** for **Name** > Click **OK**.

8.   Select **Fixed Constraint** > Select the face as shown > Click **OK**

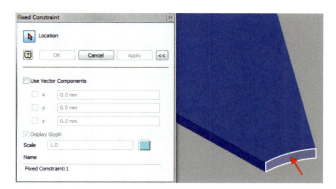

9.   Select **Body Loads** > Select **Angular** tab > Select **Enable Angular Velocity and Acceleration** > Select the face to specify the direction of the fan speed > Specify 2000rpm > Click **OK**

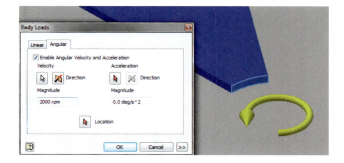

Specifying rpm after the value will convert the value into the default degrees/s.

If the complete Fan was analyzed, the boundary condition specified in step 8 and 9 would suffice. However, as we are only modeling a single blade, we need to specify extra boundary conditions to enable it to behave like a complete model. This can be achieved by applying frictional constraints on all faces that are created as a result of the **Split** feature.

CHAPTER 2
DP1 – Cyclic Symmetry Analysis

Specify symmetry conditions

10. Select **Frictionless Constraint** > Select all eight faces on the split planes > Specify **Cyclic Symmetry** for **Name** > Click **OK**

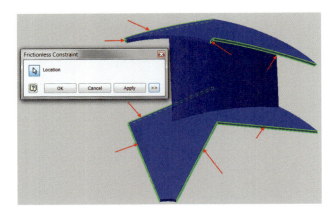

11. Select **Mesh View**

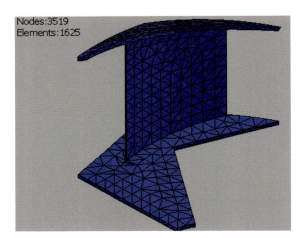

📝 A complete model would create many more elements, as illustrated below;

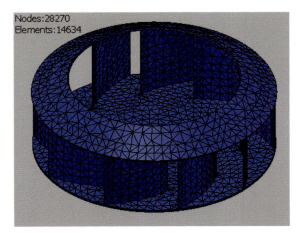

Run simulation and analyze

12. Select **Simulate** > Run **Analysis**

13. Select **Actual for Displacement Display** > Deselect **Mesh View**

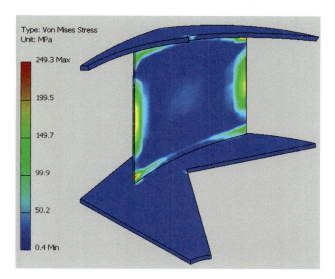

📝 Stress singularities will appear at the blade and plate interface due to sudden geometrical discontinuities and will be ignored as the area of interest is in the middle of the blades.

📝 Stress singularites may also occur in the area of the split faces and can be ignored as they would have not appeared if the complete fan would have been analyzed.

14. Select **Color Bar** > Unselect **Maximum** > Specify **200**MPa > Click **OK**

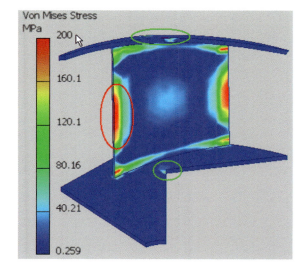

💡 Use Color bar to pinpoint the stress display in the area of interest and to enhance the stress display

SECTION 2 - Stress Analysis Design Problems using Solid Elements

CHAPTER 2

DP1 – Cyclic Symmetry Analysis

As we are interested in the middle of the blade, we can use **Probe** to display stresses in the area of interest to us.

15. Select **Probe** > Select in the middle of the blade at the front and rear > Deselect **Probe** to end Probe command

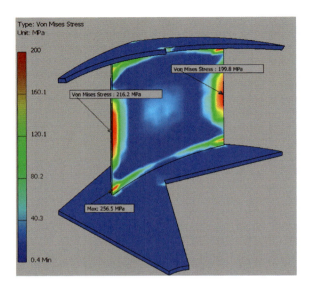

 Zoom into the area of interest before using the Probe

> **IMPORTANT** – The exact stress value of **Probe** is dependent on the location clicked; hence, the value may slightly differ

Below is stress plot of a complete model, illustrating similar stresses in all the blades of the fan

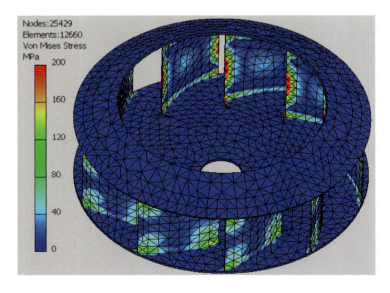

Manual convergence of results

Now, we will increase the mesh to see whether the stress results changes in the blades

16. Select **Mesh Settings** > Change **Average Element Size** to **0.05** > Click **OK**

17. Right click **Mesh** > Select **Update Mesh** > Select **Mesh View**

Reducing the average element size can have a significant impact on the size of the mesh.

Reducing the average element size from 0.1 to 0.05 has increased the number of elements by 298% and it will thus take a longer to run the simulation.

18. Rerun **Simulation** > Deselect **Mesh View**

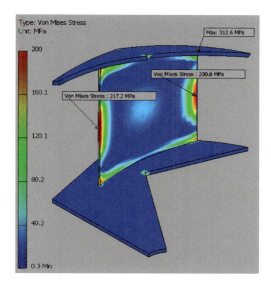

Although the maximum stress has moved to back of blade and increased, the stress in the middle of the blade has only changed to 217.2MPa, which is less than 1%. Use your **Probe** values for comparison.

CHAPTER 2
DP1 – Cyclic Symmetry Analysis

To confirm whether this stress in the middle of the blade has converged, we will rerun one more analysis with a smaller element size.

19. Select **Mesh Settings** > Change average Element Size to **0.025** > Click **OK**

20. Right click **Mesh** > Select **Update Mesh** > Select **Mesh View**

Reducing the average element size from 0.1 to 0.025 has increased the number of element by 2,160%. The number of elements may slightly differ

A full model with similar mesh size of 0.025 will create 164,680 elements as illustrated.

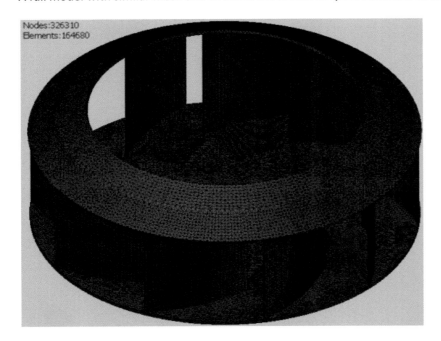

21. Run **Simulation** > Deselect **Mesh View**

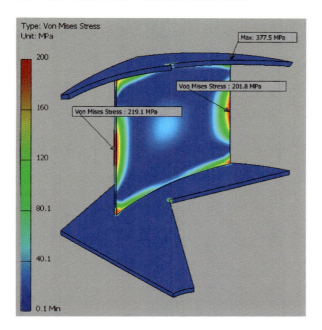

Ignore the maximum stress as it is occurring on the top plate and blade interface due to geometrical discontinuities leading to stress singularities.

Probe positions can be altered by right clicking and selecting **Edit Position** as shown below

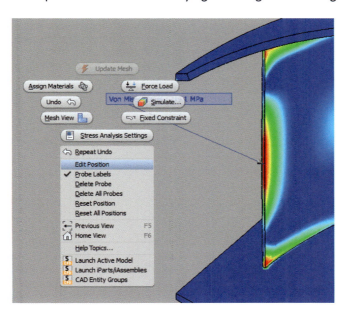

By changing the position, you can display the results in different areas of the model.

CHAPTER 2

DP1 – Cyclic Symmetry Analysis

Alternatively, you can select multiple areas of the model with the **Probe** option.

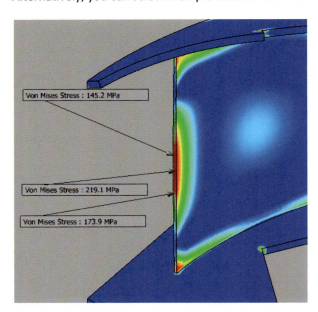

The maximum value in the middle of the blade does not exceed 219MPa. As we are only interested in this region, we can confidently say that the results have converged in the area of interest.

22.   Deselect **Probe Labels** > Double click **Displacement** from the **Stress Analysis** browser

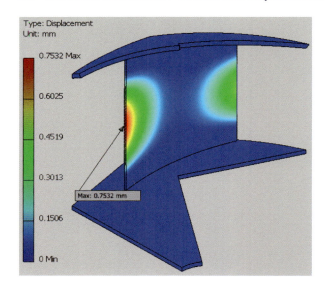

The maximum deformation plots for mesh settings of 0.1 and 0.05 are also shown below

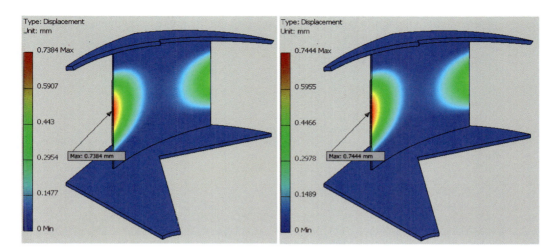

The maximum deflection occurs in the middle of the blade and changes from 0.7405 to 0.7538, a change of 1.8%, such that the displacement values can also be treated as having converged. The values may slightly differ.

23. Select **Probe Labels** > Double Click **Safety Factor**

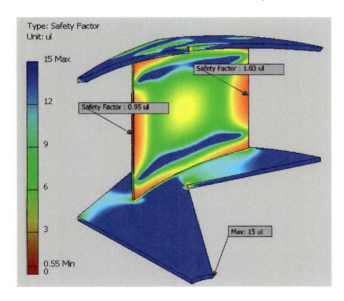

Use the color bar to adjust range.

Based on the stress in the middle of the blade (214MPa), we have a safety factor below 1, which suggests that the design has failed as the design limit is 1.5. In the next section, we will perform an optimization study to meet the design limits.

Optimization

In this section, we will alter blade thickness from 2 to 5mm using the parametric study and manually alter the material from mild steel to high strength steel.

24. Right Click **Single-Blade** > Select **Copy Simulation**

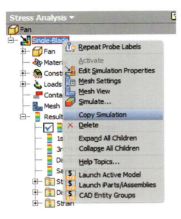

25. Right Click copied **Single-Blade:1** > Select **Edit Simulation Properties**

26. Specify **Blade-Optimization** for **Name** > Select **Parametric Dimension** for **Design Objective** > Click **OK**

This will, now, allow us to carry out a parametric study.

Investigate the affect of the thickness of the fan blade

27. Right Click **Fan.ipt** in the browser > Select **Show Parameters**

28. Select the **bladethickness** user parameter > Click **OK**

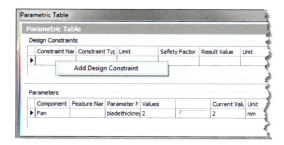

29. Select **Parametric Table**

30. Right Click in the **Design Constraints** row > Select **Add Design Constraint**

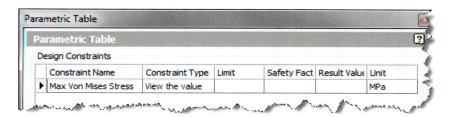

31. Select **Von Mises Stress from the list > Click OK**

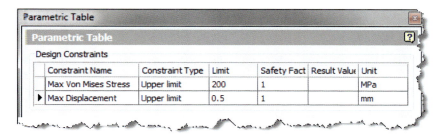

32. Repeat step **30** to add **Displacement** design constraints

33. Change the **Constraint Type** for Max Von Mises Stress to **Upper Limit** > Specify limit as **200**

34. Change the **Constraint Type** for Max Displacement to **Upper Limit** > Specify limit as 0.5

35. Specify 2-5:4 in the Bladethickness **Values** field

 This will generate values of 2, 3, 4, 5 such that three additional parameters will be created

36. Right Click anywhere in the parameter rows and select **Generate Range Configurations**

37. Move slider to see the blade changing its thickness > Specify **2** for **Current Value** > Click **Close**

38. Select **Mesh Settings** > Specify **0.05** for **Average Element Size** > Click **OK**

39. Select **Mesh View**

40. Select **Simulate** > Run **Simulation**

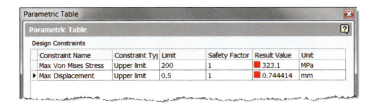 This will run four analyzes for blade thickness values of 2,3,4 and 5

41. Select **Actual** for **Displacement Scale** > Deselect **Mesh View**

42. Select **Parametric Table**

The red icon indicates unacceptable parameters based on the constraint limits

Constraint Name	Constraint Typ	Limit	Safety Factor	Result Value	Unit
Max Von Mises Stress	Upper limit	200	1	🟥 323.1	MPa
▶ Max Displacement	Upper limit	0.5	1	🟥 0.744414	mm

The Max Von Mises Stress value is also misleading as this value represents stress singularities in the model. To synchronize the stress limit with the model, change the color bar range between 0 and 200.

43. Select **Color Bar** > Specify **200** for **Maximum** value > Click **OK**

Now compare the color plots as you move the slider between 2 and 5. From the color plots, blade thickness values 4 and 5 do not show any red color in the blades, indicating low stress, with thickness 5 showing the least stress.

44. Move the slider to read a value of **5** > Select **Close**

We will now use the probe to determine the exact value of stress in the middle of blade

45. Select **Probe** and select Blade at the highest stress point > Deselect **Probe**

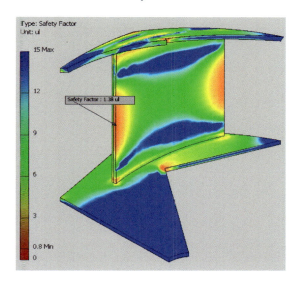 You may need to select several locations to get an indication of the highest Stress point

46. Double click **Safety Factor**

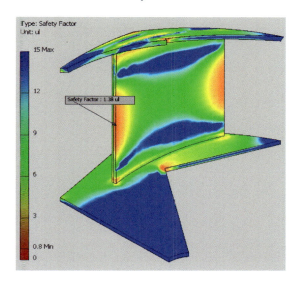

The safety factor is still below the design limit of 1.5, so we will now assign a new material

Change material

47. Select **Assign Material**

48. Select **Steel**, **High Strength Low Alloy** from the **Override Material** list > Click **OK**

49. Select **Parametric Table** > Move the slider to read **Current Value** of **5**

CHAPTER 2
DP1 – Cyclic Symmetry Analysis

50. Right click the slider > Select **Simulate this configuration** > Select **Run**

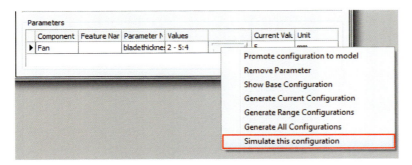

51. Double Click **Safety Factor**

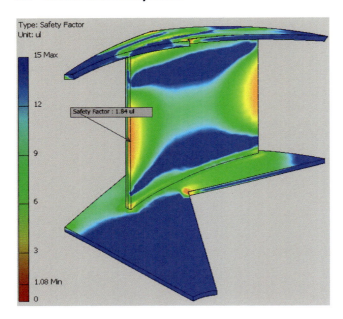

Now, by changing the material, we have reached our goal of having a safety factor above 1.5 and a max displacement below 0.5 mm. Ignore maximum stress as it is occurring on the top plate; in reality, this does not exist. Refer to the stress display of the complete fan shown earlier.

52. Close the file

DP2 – Assembly Optimization

Structural Optimization of a Lifting Mechanism
(Design Problem courtesy of Unipart Rail Ltd)

Key features and workflows introduced in this design problem

	Key Features/Workflows
1	Assembly contacts - Manual and Automatic
2	Local mesh refinement
3	Planar X,Y,Z stress plots
4	Parametric optimization

Introduction

Unipart Rail is part of Unipart Group, one of Europe's leading independent logistic companies, employing more than 9,000 people worldwide with annual turnover of more than £1.1 billion.

Unipart Rail combines extensive engineering, logistic, and manufacturing experience with industry-leading supply chain & lean expertise.

Bogie Secondary Suspension System

CHAPTER 3
DP2 – Assembly Optimization

Autodesk Inventor is used within the design & development division of Unipart Rail to produce, validate and document complete digital prototypes. In addition, the simulation suite is used extensively, making it possible to optimize, validate, and predict how designs will work under real-world conditions, before the product or part is even built.

Within Unipart Rail's bogie overhaul facility at Doncaster, UK, there is a requirement for the design of innovative jigs and fixtures in order to facilitate lean processes. One such requirement identified is the need for a lifting devise to handle the secondary suspension units fitted to the rail vehicle bogies as illustrated below. There are two secondary suspension units per bogie, each weighing 78Kg.

In this design problem, we need to determine the structural integrity of the lifting mechanism in addition to the following:

1. The maximum working stress in the key components.
2. The maximum deflection.
3. How to reduce the overall weight.

- Material to be used is mild steel
- Factor of Safety to be at least 4

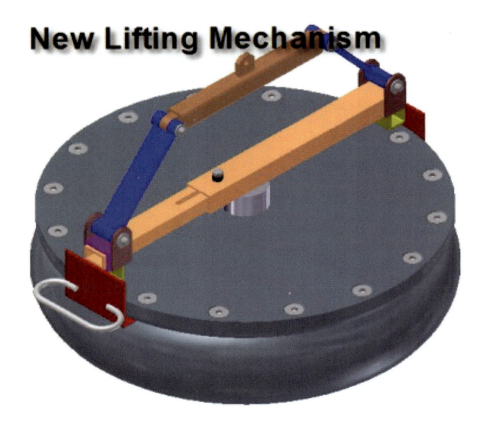

Workflow of Design Problem 2

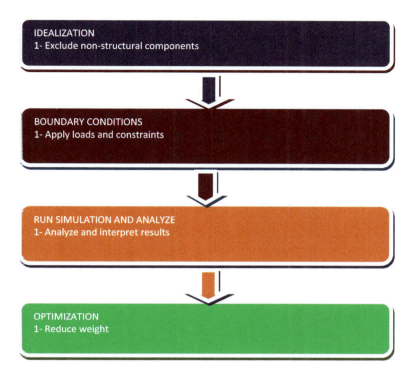

Idealization

In this stage of the FEA workflow, the components and assemblies need to be simplified in terms of having non structural features, including holes and fillets to be suppressed. In this design problem, most of the non-critical fillet features have already been suppressed.

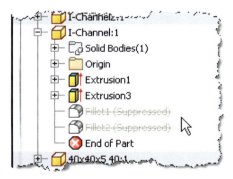

Further, nonstructural components will not be suppressed but instead will be excluded from the simulation within the Stress Analysis environment.

CHAPTER 3

DP2 – Assembly Optimization

1. Open *Airbag lifting jig*.iam

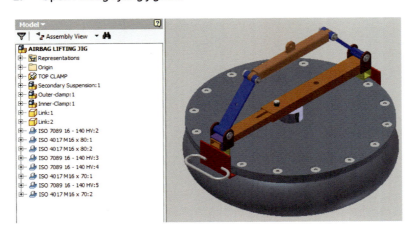

2. Select **Environments** tab > Select **Stress Analysis**

3. Select **Create Simulation** > Specify **Optimization-Study** for **Name** > Select **Parametric Dimension** for **Design Objective** > Specify **0.3**mm for **Tolerance** > Click **OK**

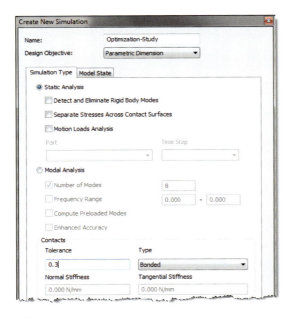

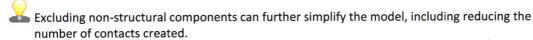 Excluding non-structural components can further simplify the model, including reducing the number of contacts created.

Changing **Tolerance** to 0.3mm will create contacts between adjacent components that have gaps of 0.3mm or less.

4.   Select the following components > Right click > Select **Exclude from Simulation**

- Secondary Suspension
- Boss
- ISO 4018 M12 x 30
- Handle
- ISO 7089 16 -140 HV:2
- ISO 7089 16 -140 HV:3
- ISO 7089 16 -140 HV:4
- ISO 7089 16 -140 HV:5

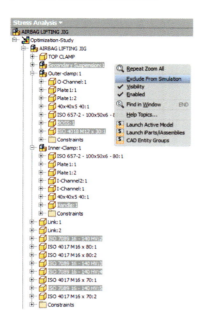

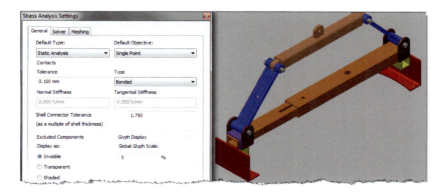

The excluded components will now become transparent.

At this stage, we can make the components invisible by altering the **Stress Analysis Settings.**

5.   Select **Stress Analysis Settings** > Select **Invisible** for **Excluded Components** > Click **OK**

The next stage is to apply boundary conditions including loads, restraints and materials.

Boundary Conditions

As the primary goal of this design problem is to determine the structural integrity of the new design, to lift the secondary suspension, we will apply its mass as a force on the new design, as it is excluded from the simulation. The following will be used to convert mass to force:

$$Force = Mass \times Acceleration$$

Were; Mass of unit is 78Kg & Acceleration (Gravity) = 10m/s^2 (Actual value is 9.81m/s^2)

Therefore, $Force = 78 \times 10 = 780N$

📝 If the suspension unit were not excluded from the simulation, there would have been no need to apply force as the weight of the unit would have been transferred via contacts.

6. Select **Force** > Select faces as shown > Specify **780** for **Magnitude** > Click **OK**

💡 Selecting both separate faces, using same **Force** command, will split the force equally to 390N on each face. Otherwise, the force would need to be halved if two forces were to be applied separately.

📝 In reality, the weight of the suspension unit will be equally distributed through the new lifting mechanism design.

7. Select **Fixed constraints** > Select the internal hole of top clamp, as shown > Click **OK**

8.   Select **Automatic Contacts**

 This will create 28 contacts in total .To easily identify contacts created between components, it is best to expand the components and assemblies within the browser as shown below.

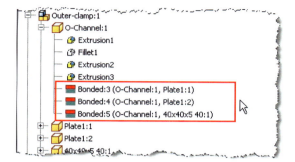

From analyzing the contacts we can see that four contacts need to be suppressed and all the contacts created between the bolts need to be changed to sliding and no separation contacts, as in reality the bolts can slide and rotate within the holes.

9.   Expand Outer-clamp:1 > Expand the 40x40x5 40:1 component > Select the Bonded: 6 & :8 contacts > Right click > Select **Suppress**.

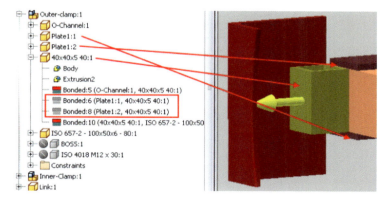

 As the adjacent faces of both components are within the 0.3mm gap, a contact has been automatically created.

Repeat step 9 for the clamp on the other side.

10. Expand Inner-clamp:1 > Expand the 40x40x5 40:1 component > Select the Bonded 13 & 16 contacts > Right click > Select **Suppress**.

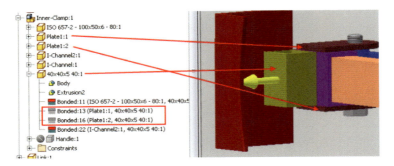

In the following steps, all bonded contacts associated with the four bolts will be changed to sliding no separation contact.

11. Expand the ISO 4017 M16 X 80:1 & 2 components > Select the contacts Bonded:14, :17, :26, :7, :9, :23 > Right click > Select **Edit Contact**

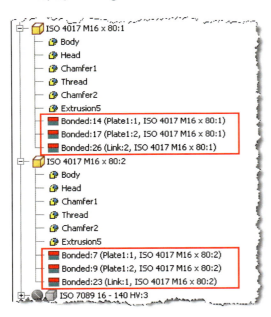

12. **Select Sliding/No separation** for **Contact type** in the **Edit contacts** dialog box > Click **OK**

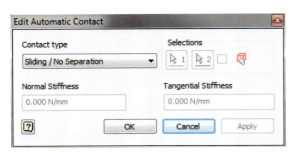

13. Expand the ISO 4017 M16 X 70:1 & 2 components > Select the contacts Bonded:1, :24, :25, :2, :27, :28 > Right Click > Select **Edit Contact**

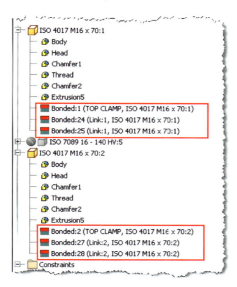

14. Select **Sliding/No separation** for **Contact type** in the **Edit contacts** dialog box > Click **OK**

In total, 12 Sliding / No Separation contacts will be created.

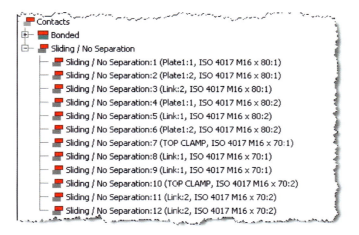

We now need to create bonded contacts between I-Channel:1 and O-Channel:1 components, as no contacts have been created between these components. This is because the gap between them is 1mm, which is higher than the default 0.3mm contact setting.

DP2 – Assembly Optimization

At this stage, we can edit the simulation properties and change the contact tolerance to 1mm, as shown below, which will create additional contacts between I-Channel:1 and O-Channel:1.

Alternatively we can create the contacts manually and for the following steps the contact will be created manually.

15. Select **Manual Contact** > Select faces of I-Channel and 0-Channel as shown > Click **OK**

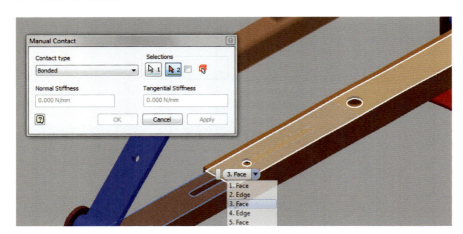

A single manual contact will be created within the bonded contact node group.

16. Select **Mesh View**

This will generate mesh and thus enable us to view the mesh so that we can further refine it if required. In this instance, the default mesh seems reasonable for the initial simulation run.

Run simulation and analyze

17. Select **Simulate** > Run **Analysis** > Deselect **Mesh View** > Select **Actual** for **Displacement Display**

 Ignore the warnings as they relate to sliding/no separation contacts, meaning that the components can slide away from one another. Hence, the software adds a soft spring to stop them sliding away.

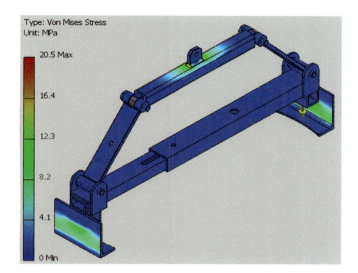

📝 The Von Mises Stress is a sum of all the planar stresses.

The maximum Von Mises Stress calculated is approximately 20.5MPa. To obtain a better understanding of the stresses in the top clamp and the plates, were the suspension unit is held, the planar stress results will be displayed.

18. Now double click Stress YY to display compressive and tensile stresses on the top clamp > Select **Color Bar** > Change the color bar maximum and minimum values to **8** and **-8** > Click **OK**

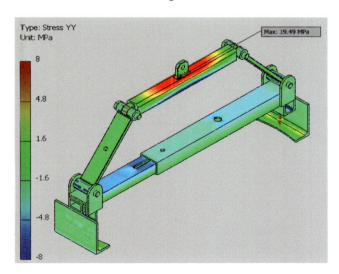

The peak stress is 19.49MPa which is concentrated around the lug. The tensile stress on the beam is in the region of 10 – 12MPa and the maximum compressive stress is approximately 9.5MPa.

📝 Use the probe to find exact value of stress on the beam.

19. Now double click **Stress ZZ** to display compressive and tensile stress on the clamp plates were the suspension unit is held

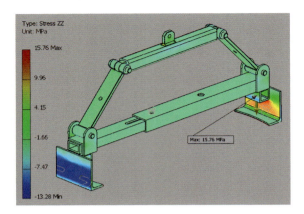

The maximum tensile stress is 15.76MPa and the maximum compressive stress is 13.49MPa

20. Now double click **Stress XX** to view the third and final planar stress

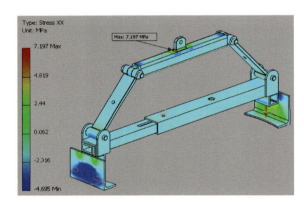

The stresses in the X plane are small when compared to the Y and Z planar stresses. As the maximum stress is at the top face of the top clamp, we will refine the mesh using a local mesh control and then compare the maximum stresses again.

 Select Constraints or Loads and then press esc key on keyboard. This will deselect results and make it easier to see selected faces when applying local mesh control

21. Select **Local Mesh Control** > Select the top face and fillet faces around lug > Specify **5**mm for element size > Click **OK**

22. Right click **Mesh** > Select **Update Mesh** > Select **Mesh View** > Select **Simulate** > Run **Analysis**

23. Double click **Stress YY**

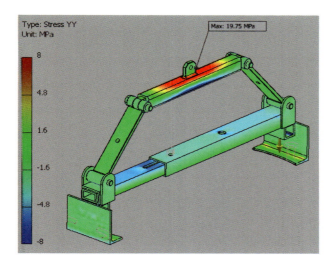

In the top clamp, the stress is significantly higher around the lug in comparison to the stress along the top clamp mount. This localized peak stress is mainly due to the geometrical discontinuity between the lug and top face of the clamp, also referred to as a stress raiser. Further mesh refinement will potentially further increase the stress due to stress singularities, due to geometrical discontinuities. In this case, as the top clamp geometry is simple and pin jointed, at either end we can treat the top clamp as simply a supported beam and thus use the following equation to calculate bending stress in the beam.

$$\sigma = Mx\frac{y}{I}$$

Load is applied centrally on the beam, therefore to find the maximum bending moment, we can use:

M = P x L / 4   y = Distance to neutral axis
  = 780N * 390mm / 4   = Section height / 2
  = 76050 Nmm   = 40mm / 2 = 20 mm

I = 2nd Moment of Area (for box section)
  = Outer 2nd Moment of Area - Inner 2nd Moment of Area
  = $(BD^3 / 12) - (bd^3 / 12)$
  = $(40 x 40^3 / 12) - (30 x 30^3 / 12)$
  = 2560000- 675000
  = 145833 mm^4

Therefore, Max Tensile or Compressive Stress due to bending is:
σ = 76050 x 20 / 145833
  = 10.43N/mm^2 = 10.43 x 10^6 N/m^2 = **10.43 MPa**

This stress calculation is based on the assumption that the maximum stress is occurring evenly in the centre of the beam. In reality, when we examine the model, we can see that the lifting lug acts as a stiffener on the beam section. Although maximum moment occurs in the centre the maximum stress will be redistributed to either side of the lug, on the upper surface of the beam.

We can see below that the section to the side of the lug marked Z-Z exhibits a maximum tensile stress on the upper face in the region of 10MPa. This is where we would expect to see the redistributed maximum tensile stress within the beam.

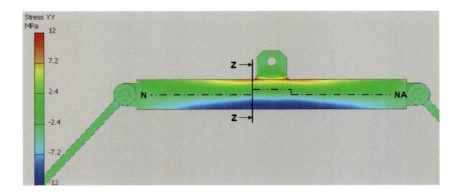

Further, as the top portion of the beam is stiffened by the lug, the neutral axis (zero stress) moves upwards, causing a greater internal moment on the underside of the beam. We would expect this to act as a stress raiser on the bottom face of the beam.
On the lower face, maximum compressive stress is still in the middle but does increase in comparison to the upper tensile stress, as expected.

These stress redistributions show good correlation between the FEA and the simple approximated hand calculation, giving us a high degree of confidence in the overall integrity of the FEA solution.

24. Double click **Displacement** to display maximum displacement

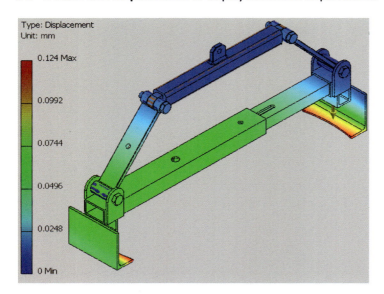

25. Double click **Safety Factor**

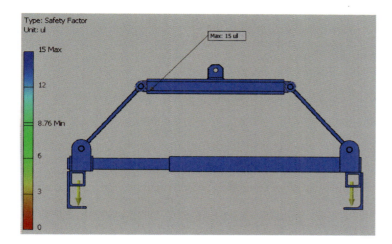

Use the color bar to enhance clarity of display. The minimum safety factor is around the lug at the top of the top clamp, as illustrated below (the position of maximum stress). Change the minimum value of the color bar to obtain a display of the safety factor results.

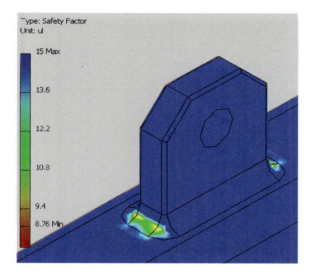

This suggests that the design can be further optimized, as the calculated safety factor of 9 is more than twice the design limit of 4.

Optimization

Here, we will use the parameters from the Component and Assembly environment and alter them to determine the best configuration that satisfies the set design constraints.

26. Select **Parametric Table**

27. Right Click in the **Design Constraints** row > Select **Add Design Constraint**

28. Select **Mass** from the list.

This will help to determine the best design/parametric configuration for minimum weight.

29. Repeat step 27 to add **Displacement** and **Safety Factor** design Constraints

30. Change the **Constraint Type** for Max Displacement to **Upper Limit** > Specify **Limit** to be **0.2**

This is the maximum allowable deflection of the assembly and a value higher than this will make the design unsuitable. At the moment, the displacement is within the limit at 0.12 mm

31. Change the **Constraint Type** for Min Safety Factor to **Lower Limit** > Specify limit to be 4

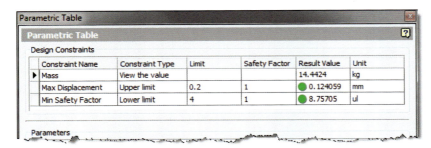

This is the minimum allowable safety factor of the assembly and a value lower than this will make the design unsuitable

> **IMPORTANT** – Only select the Linkthickness parameter in the following steps if you do not have a powerful machine.

32. Right Click Link:1 > Select **Show Parameters** > Select the following user parameters > Click **OK**

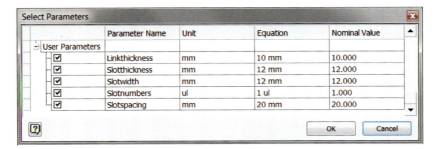

SECTION 2 - Stress Analysis Design Problems using Solid Elements

The Linkthickness parameter will allow us see the effect of changing the thickness of the link arms.

The Slotthickness and Slotwidth parameters together allow us to control the shape of the cutouts in the link arms. The shape of the cutout can be either a slot or circle.

The Slotnumbers parameter will allow us to control the number of weight-saving cutouts in the Link arms.

The Slotspacing parameter will allow us to control the spacing between weight-saving cutouts in the Link arms.

33.   Select Parametric Table, if not already selected.

Parametric Table

Design Constraints

Constraint Name	Constraint Type	Limit	Safety Factor	Result Value	Unit
▶ Mass	Minimize			14.4425	kg
Max Displacement	Upper limit	0.2	1	● 0.124041	mm
Min Safety Factor	Lower limit	4	1	● 8.75846	ul

Parameters

Component N	Feature Name	Parameter Nar	Values		Current Value	Unit
▶ Link		Linkthickness	10		10	mm
Link		Slotthickness	12		12	mm
Link		Slotwidth	12		12	mm
Link		Slotnumbers	1		1	ul
Link		Slotspacing	20		20	mm

All selected parameters now appear in addition to the design constraints, both of which can be used for the optimization study.

The weight of the lifting mechanism can be reduced by using any of the above combination parameters including thickness of link arms, number of weight-saving holes and the size.

34.   Specify 4,6,9,10 in the Linkthickness **Values** field

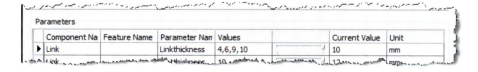

Parameters

Component Na	Feature Name	Parameter Nam	Values		Current Value	Unit
▶ Link		Linkthickness	4,6,9,10		10	mm
Link		thickness	10		12	mm

This will only generate the specified parameters

CHAPTER 3

DP2 – Assembly Optimization

35. Specify the following values to complete the parametric table

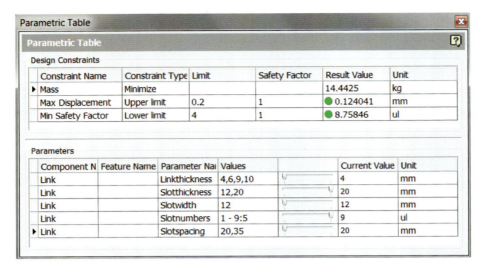

 1-9:5 will produce three more parameters, equally spaced between 1 and 9. Here, the additional parameters created are 3, 5 and 7.

Choosing too many parameters and values can result in taking a long time to generate and produce results.

 It's better to check parameters configurations within the Assembly Environment before generating them in the Simulation Environment.

 It is more effective to select **Generate Range Configurations** by selecting each row individually.

36. Right click anywhere in the parameter rows and select **Generate all Configurations**

37. Now move the slider to see the effect of the parameters changes on the lifting mechanism

38. Select **Simulate** > Select **Run**

Selecting the **Exhaustive set of configurations** option can result in taking a long time to analyze, if all parameters are selected.

 Select **Smart set configurations** and, for configurations that have not been calculated, you can individually create configurations by moving the slider, and then select **Simulate this configuration.**

39. Now move the slider to see the effect of the parameters on the design constraints

40. Finally select **Minimize** in the **Constraint Type** for **Mass** and see the parameter configuration selected

41. Right Click anywhere on any the **Parameter** rows > Select **Simulate this Configuration**. This will generate visual results, to take account of the selected parameter values.

Here you can further add more parameters, change design constraint limits, etc., to further optimize the design.

Based on which parameters are chosen, which are entirely dependent on the designer, any of the following design configurations can be achieved.

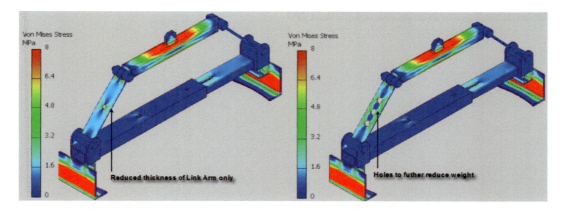

The number of design configurations is unlimited and the above configurations can be further enhanced by adding more holes and reducing the thickness of the other channels of the lifting mechanism.

 Based on engineering intuition you can manually move the sliders to the desired values and then right click anywhere on the parameter rows and then select simulate this configuration.

CHAPTER 3

DP2 – Assembly Optimization

Another possible configuration is illustrated below.

However, it is important to note that selection of the design is dependent on various criteria including manufacturability, company/designer preferences, best practices etc.

42. Close File

DP3 – Bolted Connection

Pre-Stressing a Bolted Clamp Assembly
(Design Problem Courtesy of Destec Engineering Ltd)

Key features and workflows introduced in this design problem

	Key Features/Workflows
1	Symmetry conditions
2	Simulating bolt preloads
3	Non-linear contacts
4	Local mesh refinement
5	Displaying symmetrical results using ground plane and reflections

Introduction

Destec Engineering Ltd was formed in 1969 and for the past 40 years has been developing both products and services to industry, particularly where design and supply is concerned, with 'High Pressure Containment' and 'On-Site Machining' being the specialist lines.

SECTION 2 - Stress Analysis Design Problems using Solid Elements

CHAPTER 4

DP3 – Bolted Connection

One of the products designed by Destec Engineering Ltd is the G-Range clamp connector, as used in the previous picture, which provides an ideal solution to piping installations, used extensively in production manifold, flow line and valve installations.

One of the key benefits of the G-Range product is it offers up to 75% weight saving over an ANSI flange. With only four bolts per joint, makes this product an easy and cost effective assembly. It is the recognized standard for clamp connectors by the Oil & Gas industry.

The main requirements of this design problem are to determine:

1. Maximum stress in the clamp assembly, for a given allowable bolt stress of 172.4MPa
2. Determine whether contact is made between seal and pipe
3. Friction will not be taken into account

Workflow of Design Problem 3

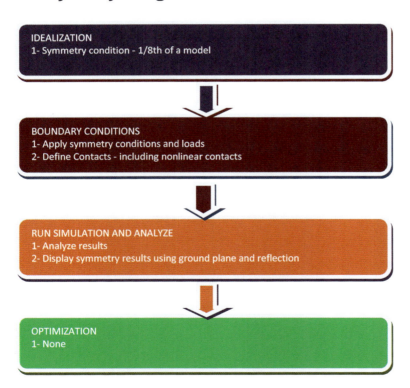

IDEALIZATION
1- Symmetry condition - 1/8th of a model

BOUNDARY CONDITIONS
1- Apply symmetry conditions and loads
2- Define Contacts - including nonlinear contacts

RUN SIMULATION AND ANALYZE
1- Analyze results
2- Display symmetry results using ground plane and reflection

OPTIMIZATION
1- None

Idealization

In this example all the bolts and the torque applied is the same meaning the stress in the bolts will be the same. As a result of this we can take advantage of symmetry conditions which will also help to run the simulation faster.

However in Inventor Simulation we cannot apply a bolt torque/preload to stress up the bolt, for this reason we will split the bolt and apply a load at the split force to simulate preload.

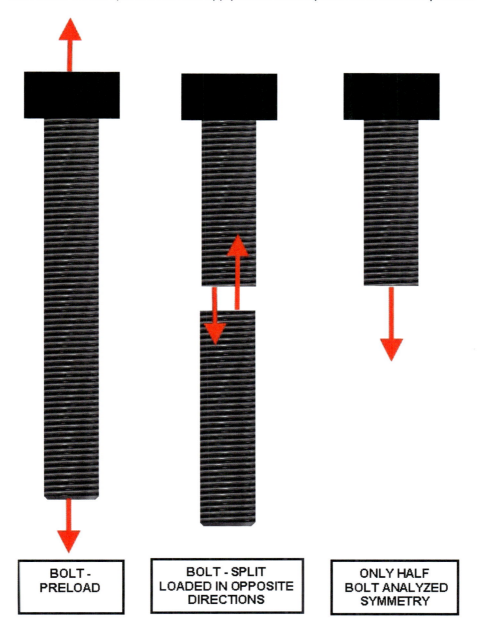

| BOLT - PRELOAD | BOLT - SPLIT LOADED IN OPPOSITE DIRECTIONS | ONLY HALF BOLT ANALYZED SYMMETRY |

CHAPTER 4

DP3 – Bolted Connection

The following equation and information will be used to determine the load to stress the bolt to a given specified value based on its diameter. This method agrees with the method given by the **American Petroleum Institute Standard API 6A**.

Bolt Size :- 1.1/8"-8UN

Nominal Bolt Size	$NB = 1.125in$
Pitch of Thread	$P = 0.125in$

Bolt Stress Area $A_b = \dfrac{\pi}{4} \cdot (NB - 1.3 \cdot P)^2$

$A_b = 0.728 \cdot in^2$ $(A_b = 469.4 \cdot mm^2)$

Assembly Bolt Stress $\sigma_b = 25000psi$ $(\sigma_b = 172.4 \cdot MPa)$

(Load on Bolt stress Area $\sigma_b \cdot A_b = $ 80912.9N)

The following information is used to calculate the bolt torque required to stress the bolt to the allowable stress.

Nominal Thread Effective Diameter $D = 1.0438in$

Half Thread Angle $\alpha = 30deg$

Coefficient of Friction $\mu = 0.12$

Inside Radius of Nut Contact Face $R_1 = \dfrac{1.25}{2} in$

Outside Radius of Nut Contact Face $R_2 = \dfrac{1.813}{2} in$

Friction Torque at Thread $A = \dfrac{\mu \cdot A_b \cdot \sigma_b \cdot D}{2 \cdot \cos(\alpha)}$

Friction Torque between Nut Face and Clamp/Cover $C = \left(2 \cdot \mu \cdot A_b \cdot \dfrac{\sigma_b}{3} \right) \cdot \dfrac{R_2^3 - R_1^3}{R_2^2 - R_1^2}$

Torque Required to Stretch Bolt Without Friction $B = \dfrac{A_b \cdot \sigma_b \cdot P}{2 \cdot \pi}$

Total Torque Required $T = (A + B + C)$

$T = 280.6 \cdot lbfft$ $(T = 380.5 \cdot N \cdot m)$

1.   Open *Bolted-Connection*.iam

2.   Activate **FEA-Symmetry** Level of Detail > Click **OK**

3.   Move **End of Features** below **1/8 Model**

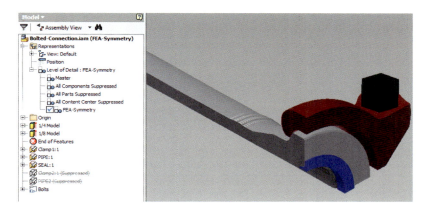

This will create 1/8th of the original model which will be used for analysis. Now, we can begin the second stage of the analysis by applying boundary conditions.

Boundary conditions

4.   Select **Environments** tab > Select **Stress Analysis**

5.   Select **Create Simulation** > Specify **Bolt-Preload** for **Name** > Click **OK**

Initially we are going to apply symmetry conditions on all the split faces, except the bolt, using frictional constraint

6. Select **Frictionless Constraint** > Select three faces as shown > Specify **Y Symmetry** for **Name** > Click **Apply**

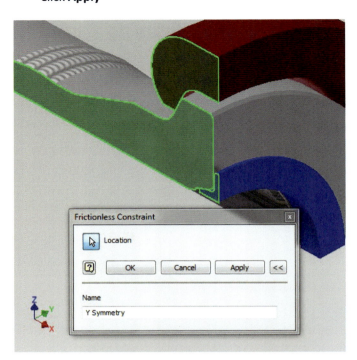

7. Now select two faces as shown > Specify **X Symmetry** for **Name** > Click **Apply**

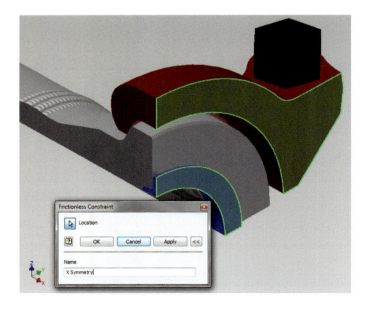

8. Finally select two faces as shown > Specify **Z Symmetry** for **Name** > Click **OK**

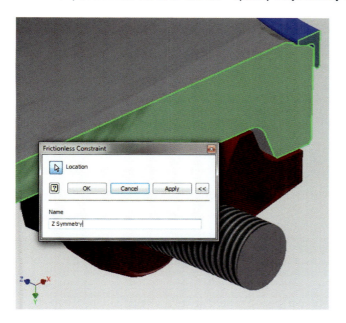

9. Select **Pressure** and specify **39.6MPa** > Select all internal exposed faces of pipe and seal > Specify **Internal Pressure** for **Name** > Click **OK**

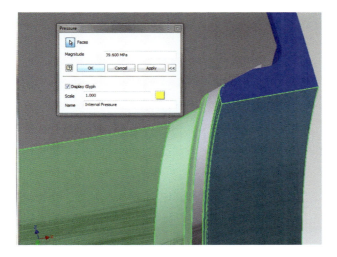

10. Select **Force** and specify **80,912.9N** > Select the bottom of the bolt split face **>** Flip the direction of Load > Specify **Bolt preload** for **Name** > Change color of load to **red** > Click **OK** twice

11. Select **Automatic Contacts** command

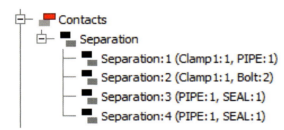

4 new contacts will be created

12. Right Click **Separation:2 (Clamp1:1,Bolt:2)** contact > Select **Edit Contact** > Select **Sliding / No Separation** for **Contact type** in the **Edit Automatic Contact** dialog box > Click **OK**

This is the contact between the clamp and bolt.

13. Right Click **Separation:1 (Clamp1:1,PIPE:1)** contact > Select **Edit Contact** > Select **Sliding / No Separation** for **Contact type** in the **Edit Automatic Contact** dialog box > Click **OK**

This is the contact between the clamp and pipe.

14. Select **Manual Contact** > Select faces of Pipe and Seal as shown > Click **OK**

This is the contact between the seal and the pipe. As the contact tolerance, defined in the simulation settings, was less than this gap the contact was not automatically created

In total 5 contacts will be created as follows

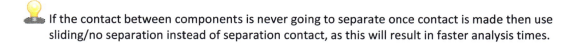 Having a lot of separation contacts in the analysis can result in long analysis runs, as these contacts are nonlinear and go through an iterative process to obtain convergence in results.

If the contact between components is never going to separate once contact is made then use sliding/no separation instead of separation contact, as this will result in faster analysis times.

Now we will set the mesh settings including local refinement around the seal.

Unselect **Use part based measure for Assembly mesh**, if already preselected, before clicking OK below. As this can result in excessive mesh elements.

15. Select **Mesh Settings** > Specify **0.02** for **Average Element Size** > Unselect **Create Curved Mesh Elements,** if already selected > Click **OK**

CHAPTER 4

DP3 – Bolted Connection

16. Select **Local Mesh Control** > Specify **1.5mm** for **Element Size** > Select the following faces which are in contact between the seal and pipe (One for pipe and two for seal) > Click **OK**

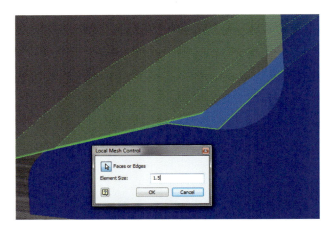

17. Select **Local Mesh Control** again > Specify **4mm** for **Element Size** > Select the following face on the seal > Click **OK**

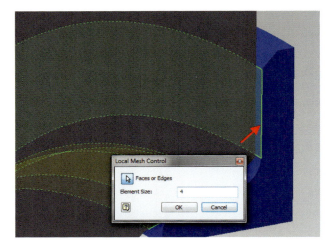

18. Select **Mesh View**

A total of 41827 elements will be created, value may differ slightly.

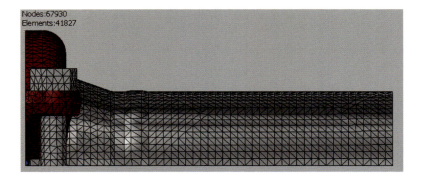

SECTION 2 - Stress Analysis Design Problems using Solid Elements

Run simulation and analyze

19. Select **Simulate** > Run **Analysis**

20. Select **Actual** for **Displacement Display** > Select **Contour Shading** > Deselect **Boundary Conditions** > Select **Show Max value** in **Display,** value may differ slightly

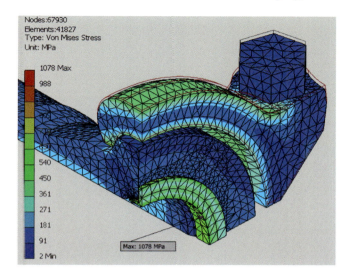

21. Zoom in to see if seal has made contact with the pipe

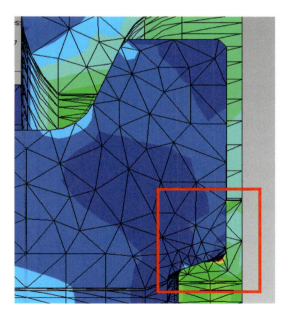

22. Select **Animate** > Select **Play** to see seal come in contact with pipe > Click **OK** once finished with animation

CHAPTER 4
DP3 – Bolted Connection

23. Select **Seal** in graphics window > Right Click and select **Isolate** > Select **Mesh View** > Select **Color Bar** > Unselect **Maximum** > Specify **900** maximum value > Click **OK**

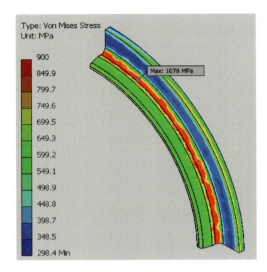

The maximum stress is way higher than the yield limit and in reality these seals are permanently deformed locally around the radii when loaded for the first time. For this reason the high stress is not an issue for the seal. What is more important, is to see whether a contact between the seal and pipe is made, as this is crucial in operation as non-contact will cause leakage.

24. Now select **SEAL:1** in graphics window > Right Click and select **Undo Isolate**

25. Select Bolt in graphics window > Right Click and select **Isolate** > Select **Color Bar** > Select **Maximum** > Click **OK**

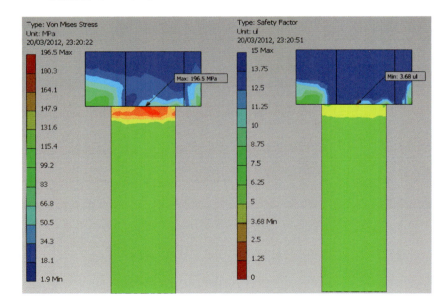

The maximum stresses in the bolt is below yield limit but it's value is different to the allowable stress of 172.4MPa. This may be down to several reasons of one which maybe down to stress singularities as the stress is very close to the edge of the bolt. The important point to note is that a minimum value of 3.68, proves the bolt is strong enough to withstand the bolt pre torque. In the case of trying to achieve a higher safety factor the results need to be carefully interpreted. Symmetry results can be further enhanced by using ground plane and reflection as illustrated below

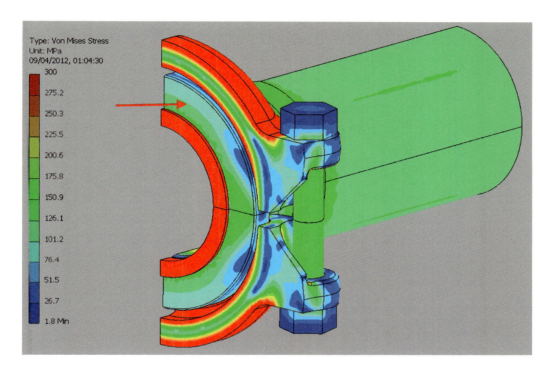

Below are some hints on how to produce above results.

1. Look at the face, indicated by the arrow in above picture, square on and then right click cube. Select Set Current View as front.

2. A Ground Plane will be created normal to the face at 0,0,0 as shown below

3. Change Displacement Display to Undeformed

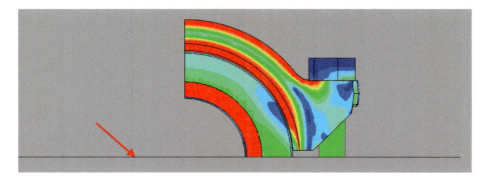

CHAPTER 4

DP3 – Bolted Connection

4. Change Reflection setting to the following values

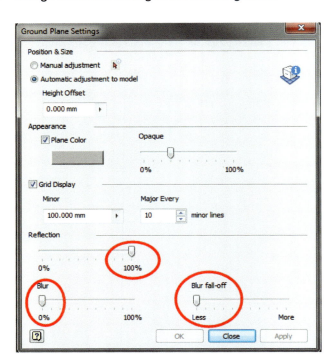

26. Close File, after viewing and analyzing results

DP4 – Weldment Analysis

Structural Design of Moving Bridge
(Design Problem Courtesy of British Waterways Ltd)

Key features and workflows introduced in this design problem

	Key Features/Workflows
1	Convert assembly to single part using **Shrinkwrap Substitute**
2	Same scale color legend display
3	Planar X,Y,Z, stress plots

Introduction

In this design problem British Waterways team where involved in designing a new Jack mechanism to open the canal bridge. The Jack force of **28,729N** was determined, using Dynamic Simulation, and will be used to validate the structural integrity of the new structure, which is to be incorporated into the existing structure beneath the bridge.

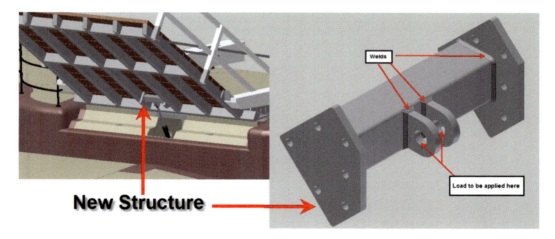

As this new structure is designed with welds incorporated as a weldment assembly, the **Export Loads to FEA** feature within Dynamic Simulation cannot be used automatically. With this in mind, we have two options.

1. Part Analysis – Convert the weldment to a single component using

   a. **Shrinkwrap** – This will convert assembly into a separate single component.
   b. **Shrinkwrap Substitute**– This will create a shrinkwrap of the assembly and creates a new substitute level of detail.

2. Assembly Analysis

CHAPTER 5

DP4 – Weldment Analysis

We will use options 1b and 2 and compare the results.

The main requirements of this design problem are to determine:

- The maximum stress in the structure whilst the bridge is being opened.
- The maximum deflection in the structure.
- The factor of safety of the new design - from which the fatigue life could be predicted.

In addition to the above requirements the design criteria to be used for this design problem are;

- Material to be used is mild steel
- Weld Material to be used is mild steel
- Minimum Factor of Safety required is 2.5

Workflow of Design Problem 4

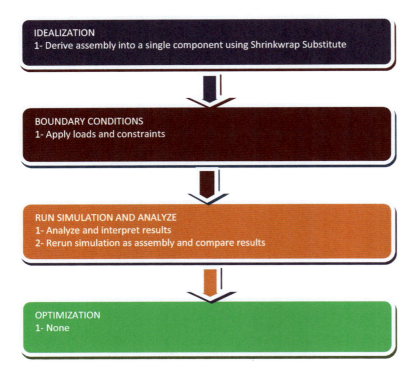

IDEALIZATION
1- Derive assembly into a single component using Shrinkwrap Substitute

BOUNDARY CONDITIONS
1- Apply loads and constraints

RUN SIMULATION AND ANALYZE
1- Analyze and interpret results
2- Rerun simulation as assembly and compare results

OPTIMIZATION
1- None

Idealization

In order to perform a comparative study between options 1b and 2, we initially need to create a single part using the **Shrinkwrap Substitute**.

1. Open *Cylinder reaction beam*.iam

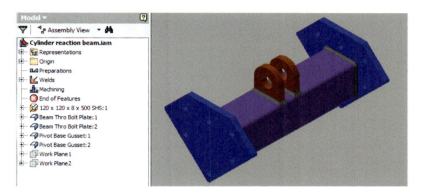

2. Right Click Level of Detail: Master > Select **New Substitute** > Select **Shrinkwrap** > Click **OK**

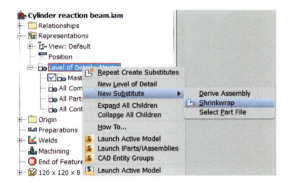

3. Select **Single Body** option >Select **None** for **Hole patching**

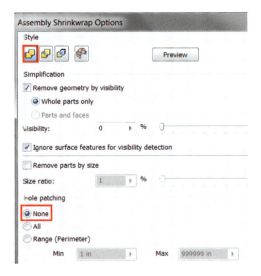

4.   Click **OK**

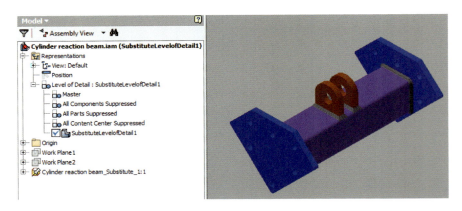

Now, we can begin the second stage of the analysis by applying boundary conditions.

Boundary conditions

5.   Select **Environments** tab > Select **Stress Analysis**

6.   Select **Create Simulation** > Specify **Shrinkwrap-Analysis** for **Name** > Click **OK**

7.   Right Click **Welds** > Select **Exclude From Simulation**

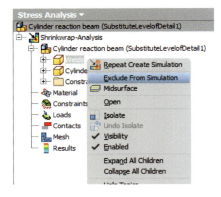

Shrinkwrap has copied the welds and hence need to exclude from simulation.

8. Select **Fixed constraints** > Select the faces on both sides as shown > Specify **Bolted-Plates** for Name > Click **OK**

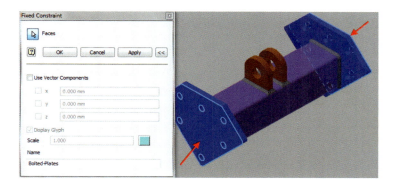

9. Select **Bearing Loads** > Select the internal circular face of both lugs to specify the location > For **Direction**, select the top face of the channel > Specify **28729N** for **Magnitude**

The force will be split for the bearing loads when both faces are selected together using the same bearing load command.

10. Specify **0.5** to reduce the force display size > Specify **Jack Reaction Load** for **Name** > Click **OK**

The newly created part has no valid material and hence we need to define the material

11. Select **Assign Materials** > Select **Steel, Mild** from the **Override Material** list > Click **OK**

12. Select **Simulate** > Run **Analysis**

13. Select the left view as shown > Select **Undeformed** for **Displacement Display** > Select **Show Max value** in **Display**

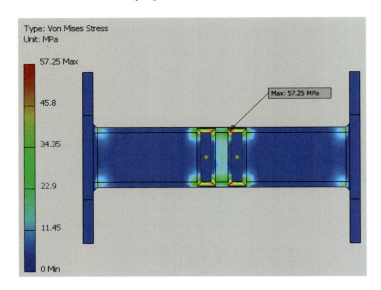

The Max Value is around the welds. Now, we will perform analysis as an assembly and then compare results

Rerun simulation as assembly and compare results

14. Right Click **Shrinkwrap-Analysis** > Select **Copy Simulation**

15. Right click **Shrinkwrap-Analysis:1** > Select **Edit Simulation Properties**

16. Specify **Weldment-Analysis** for **Name** > Select **Model State** tab > Select **Master** for **Level of Detail** > Click **OK.**

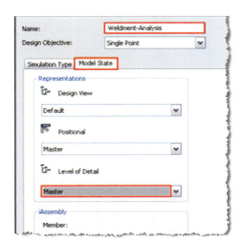

The welds will be suppressed from the simulation

17. Right click **Welds** > Reselect **Exclude from Simulation**

The welds are now included in the simulation.

18. Right click **Contacts** > Select **Update Automatic Contacts**

A total of 38 contacts will be created within the Weldment Assembly.

- Bonded:33 (Welds, 120 x 120 x 8 x 500 SHS:1)
- Bonded:34 (Welds, Beam Thro Bolt Plate:2)
- Bonded:35 (120 x 120 x 8 x 500 SHS:1, Beam Thro Bolt Plate:1)
- Bonded:36 (120 x 120 x 8 x 500 SHS:1, Beam Thro Bolt Plate:2)
- Bonded:37 (120 x 120 x 8 x 500 SHS:1, Pivot Base Gusset:1)
- Bonded:38 (120 x 120 x 8 x 500 SHS:1, Pivot Base Gusset:2)

Using fillets will increase the number of contacts produced. For example, the channel below with round edges will result in eight extra contacts.

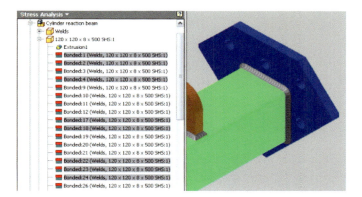

Suppress fillets to reduce the number of contacts produced.

We will continue this design problem without suppressing the fillets, as the assembly is small.

19. Right click **Bolted-Plates** constraint > Select **Edit Fixed Constraints** > Reselect the faces to apply the fixed constraint > Click **OK**

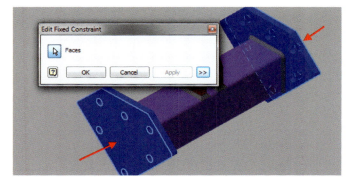

SECTION 2 - Stress Analysis Design Problems using Solid Elements

CHAPTER 5
DP4 – Weldment Analysis

20. Right click **Jack Reaction** Load > Select **Edit Bearing Load** > Reselect the faces to reapply bearing load and direction, as shown below > Click **OK**

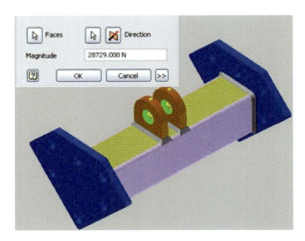

It is necessary to reapply the loads and constraints as the model has changed from a part to an assembly.

21. Select **Mesh View**

Run simulation and analyze

22. Select **Simulate** > Run **Analysis**

23. Select **Actual** for **Displacement Display** > Select **Show Max value** in **Display**

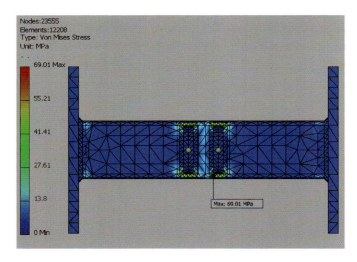

Max value may slightly differ.

Note the stress is higher than the shrink-wrapped component by 11MPa. This is normally due to sliver (or highly distorted) mesh elements between the welds and the components. So, when analyzing weldments, be aware of the sliver elements distorting results.

To gain some confidence in the accuracy of the results, the mesh needs to be refined either by using a smaller global average element size or refining the mesh around the weld areas only using local mesh control. The latter method will be used.

24. Deselect **Show Max value** > Deselect **Mesh View**, if mesh is visible

Select Constraints or Loads and then press esc key on keyboard. This will deselect results and make it easier to see selected faces when applying local mesh control

25. Select **Local Mesh Control** > Specify **5mm** > Select all eight weld faces > Select four vertical faces of the lugs > Click **OK**

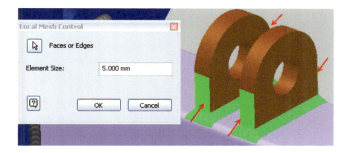

26. Right Click **Mesh** > Select **Update Mesh**

27. Select **Mesh View**

28. Select **Simulate** > Rerun **Analysis**

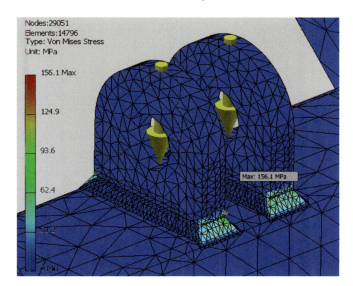

The maximum stress has now increased to 156.1MPa. This significant increase is due to stress singularities caused by sharp discontinuity in the geometrical shape around the welds. Using automatic convergence will also not result in convergence of results.

SECTION 2 - Stress Analysis Design Problems using Solid Elements

CHAPTER 5

DP4 – Weldment Analysis

At this stage we can try to further idealize the model by removing the sharp edges around the welds by introducing fillets.

29. Select **Finish Stress Analysis** > Double click **Master Level of Detail** > Double click Pivot Base Gusset:1

30. Introduce **Fillet1** by moving **End of Folded** to the end > Select **Return**

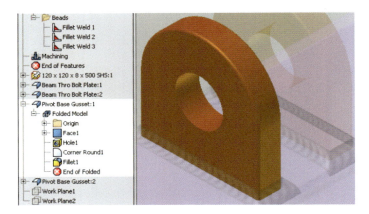

31. Expand Welds node > Double click **Fillet Weld 3** > Reselect component 2 of weld bead > Select both lugs > Click **OK**

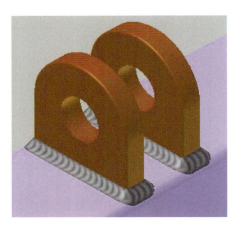

32. Select **Environments** tab > Select **Stress Analysis**

33. Expand Mesh node > Right click **Local Mesh:1** > Select **Delete** to remove mesh control

34. Right click **Contacts** > Select **Update Automatic Contacts**

35. Right click **Mesh** > Select **Update Mesh**

36. Select **Simulate** > Run **Analysis**

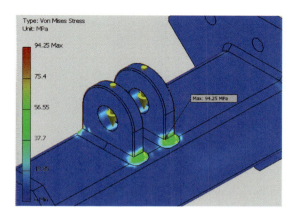

Max value may differ. Although the stress has reduced slightly to 94.25MPa, we still cannot gain convergence in the results due to stress singularities. In these scenarios, by manipulating the color display, we can visualize the area of stress singularities.

37. Select **Color Bar** > Unselect **Maximum** > Specify **55**MPa > Click **OK** > Deselect **Mesh View** > Deselect **Maximum Value** > Click **OK**

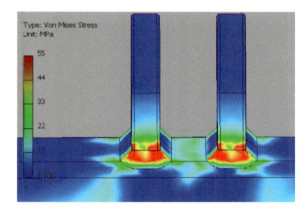

To obtain further confidence in the results, we can analyze the X,Y and Z planar stresses.

38. Double click **Stress XX**

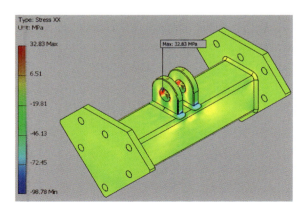

CHAPTER 5

DP4 – Weldment Analysis

By displaying the Stress XX plot, we have noticed the maximum stress value of around 98MPa is a compressive stress and the maximum tensile stress of around 33MPa is located in the area were the load is applied. It is important to note here that the compressive strength of most materials is higher than the tensile strength, which means the tensile stress becomes the area of the concern rather than the compressive stress.

39. Double click **Stress YY**

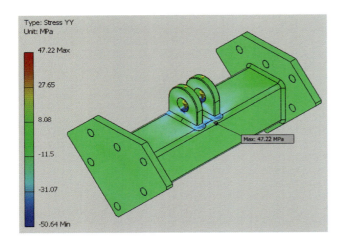

40. Right click **120x120x8x500 SHS:1** > Select **Isolate** to view results of the channel only

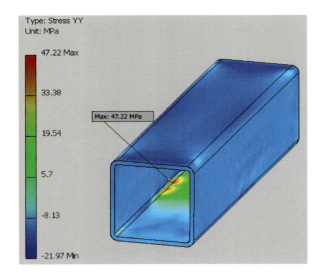

41. Select Same Scale

SECTION 2 - Stress Analysis Design Problems using Solid Elements

Same Scale does not alter the range of the color bar even when you are looking at individual components in isolation. So, it helps to compare results visually.

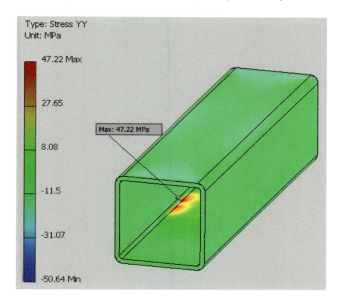

The above image illustrates that the maximum tensile stress of 47MPa is located inside the channel, directly beneath the lugs.

42.   Double click **Stress ZZ**

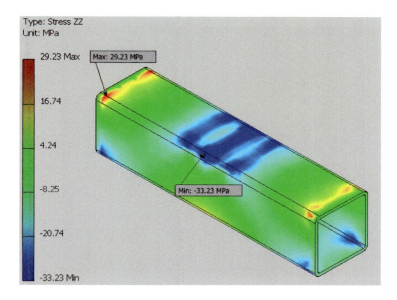

43. Reselect **Undo Isolate** > Double click **Safety Factor**

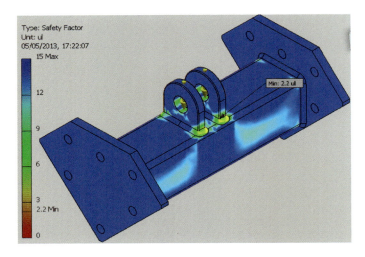

The minimum factor of safety is calculated based on the maximum stress of 96.91MPa Hence,

$$Factor\ of\ Safety = \frac{205}{94.21} = 2.17$$

Based on the single shrinkwrapped component

$$Factor\ f\ Safety = \frac{205}{57.25} = 3.58$$

So take care in manipulating results. By adjusting the color bar, we can display the minimum factor of safety as illustrated.

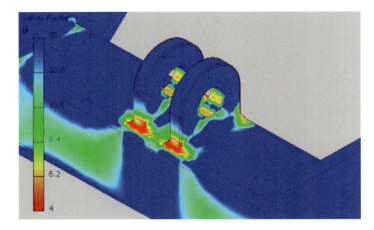

44. Close File

DP5 – Assembly Analysis with built-in welds

Structural Validation of Trailer Chassis
(Design Problem courtesy of Wright Resolutions Ltd)

Key features and workflows introduced in this design problem

	Key Features/Workflows
1	Automatic bonded contacts - Welded fabricated structure analysis
2	Multiple-loads
3	Planar X,Y,Z, stress plots
4	Interpretation of results with stress singularities present

Introduction

Wright Resolutions Ltd is a design consultancy specializing in agricultural cultivation and crop establishment machinery. Current clients include a number of well known UK and European agricultural machinery manufacturers.

As part of a project to design a new concept for a trailer chassis, it was necessary to determine the loadings on and strength/deflections of a conventionally manufactured trailer chassis, as can be seen in the following picture. Such chassis are generally manufactured from hollow section steel together with flame-cut steel plates and flat bar parts.

CHAPTER 6

DP5 - Assembly Analysis with built-in welds

Initially, the trailer was modeled in Dynamic Simulation to determine the loads at all critical areas including the drawbar, axle spring mountings, tipping cylinder, and rear hinges to the body. Maximum load situations during tipping were then taken and applied via FEA to determine the parameters listed below. One such situation, simplified, is used for this design problem.

The requirements of this design problem are to determine:

1. The maximum compressive and tensile stresses in the chassis.
2. The maximum deflection of the chassis under load.
3. The factor of safety.
4. The key stress zones for potential reinforcement when designing an alternative chassis.

In addition to the above requirements, the design criteria to be used for this design problem are as follows.

1. Material to be used is EN 50D / S355J2G3 steel.
2. Factor of safety required is 1.5.

Workflow of Design Problem 5

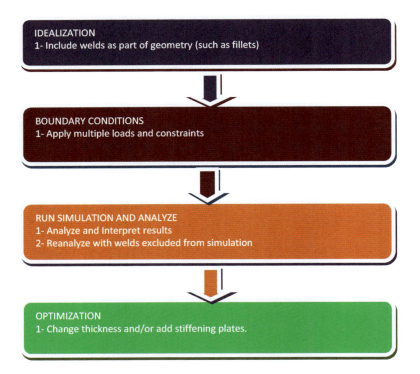

Part 1-Chassis design with Welds and RHS Channel Radii

Idealization

To simplify the analysis of the fabricated chassis, the welds have been modeled as fillets within the components, which will greatly help to reduce the number of contacts produced.

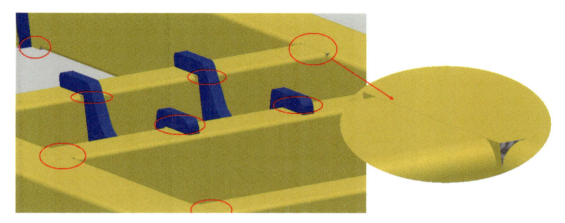

As the strength and characteristics of RHS are dependent on the corner radii, it is important to include these for more meaningful results. If welds are modeled separately to the RHS, the joints created in FEA are often complex and can be based on very thin slivers (highly distorted mesh elements) at the limits of the corner radii. Stress singularities produced can be very high. In practice, provided that the welds are correct and homogenous to the sections to which they are applied, such slivers are not present. Extruding the weld as part of the original section can represent nearer to a realistic situation. *It is important to simulate welds in a manner that represents reality, as close as possible, for the results to be meaningful.* The use of filler materials to bridge over the joints, or partial V butt welds, for example, would alter the strength and integrity of the structure in practice and lead to different results from those simulated.

1.   Open *Chassis*.iam

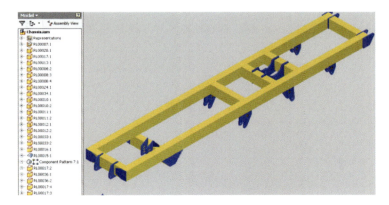

2.   Select **Environments** tab > Select **Stress Analysis**

3.   Select **Create Simulation** > Specify **Chassis-Analysis** for **Simulation Name** > Click **OK.**

CHAPTER 6
DP5 - Assembly Analysis with built-in welds

Boundary conditions

4.   Select **Automatic** contacts to detect adjacent faces between components and welds

A total of 100 contacts will be created within the weldment assembly.

📝 Many more contacts would have been created if the welds had been modeled separately as a weldment assembly.

The chassis is attached to the tractor via a drawbar arm, which is secured to the chassis via locking pins. Therefore, we will apply pin constraints to secure the chassis

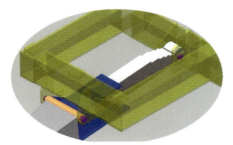

5.   Select **Pin Constraint** > Select the faces of both holes as shown > Click Apply

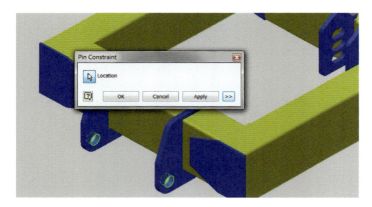

6.   Now select the back faces of the two middle slots as shown > Click **OK**

With the aid of Dynamic Simulation, the trailer is used to simulate tipping to determine the maximum reaction forces on the chassis.

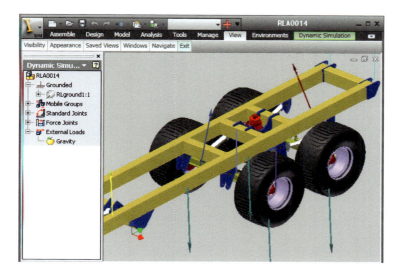

As the loads cannot be exported automatically, because this function only supports single parts, we will specify these bearing loads manually.

First, we will apply the forces generated by the load and weight of chassis.

7.   Select **Gravity** > Select **Use Vector Components** > Specify **-9810** in the Z direction > Click **OK**

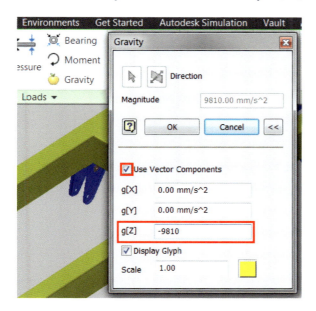

As there are many bearing loads to be applied, we will select multiple bearing load faces, lying on the same axis, to help speed up the creation of loads. As the bearing loads are split equally by the number of faces selected, we will simply multiply the actual loads by the number of faces selected. Alternatively, you can create a load on each individual face.

CHAPTER 6

DP5 - Assembly Analysis with built-in welds

8.   Select **Bearing Load** > Select two internal circular faces as shown below > Specify the top face of the plate as the **Direction** of the force > Specify **280,000** for **Magnitude**

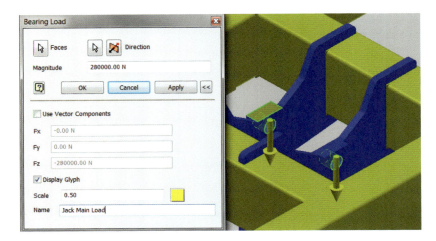

9.   Specify **0.5** to reduce size of the force display > Specify **Jack Main Load** for **Name** > Click **Apply**

10. Now select the two internal circular faces of the bushings as shown > Specify top face of plate to specify the **Direction** of the force as shown > Specify **50,000** for **Magnitude**

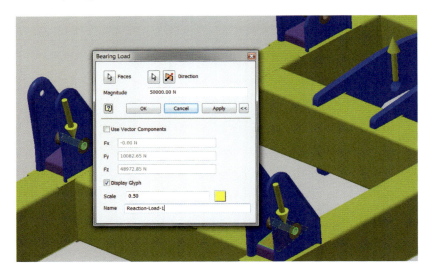

11. Specify **Reaction-load-1** for **Name** > Click **Apply**

12. Now select the two internal circular faces of the bushings as shown > Specify the top face of plate to specify the **Direction** of force, as shown > Specify **82000** for **Magnitude**

13. Specify **Reaction-load-2** for **Name** > Click **Apply**

14. Now select the two internal circular faces of the bushings as shown > Specify the top face of the plate to specify the **Direction** of force as shown > Specify **58000** for **Magnitude**

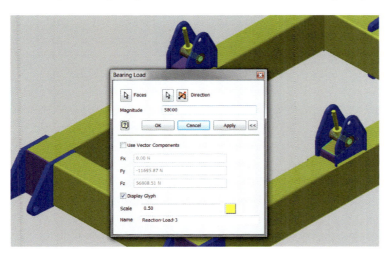

15. Specify **Reaction-load-3** for **Name** > Click **Apply**

16. Now select the four internal circular faces of the bushings as shown below > Specify the top face of the chassis to specify the **Direction** of force, as shown > Specify **84000** for **Magnitude**

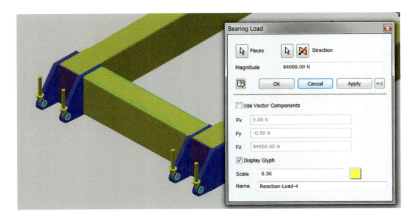

17. Specify **Reaction-load-4** for **Name** > Click **OK**

18. Select **Mesh Setting** > Specify **0.025** for **Average Element Size** > Unselect **Use part based measure for Assembly mesh** > Click **OK**

19. Select **Mesh View**

 141,088 elements are generated. Leaving **Use part based measure for Assembly mesh** selected would have created more elements.

Run simulation and analyze

20. Select **Simulate** > Run **Analysis**

21. Deselect **Mesh View** > Select **Undeformed** for **Displacement Display** > Select **Show Max value in Display** > Deselect **Boundary Conditions**

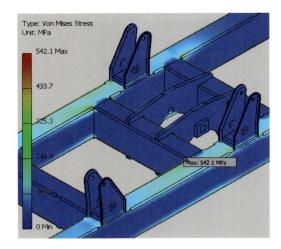

Max Stress value may differ

The maximum stress value is around the weld areas, and mounts, and is largely due to stress singularities as a result of discontinuity in the geometrical shape. Refining the mesh around these areas will not necessarily reduce stresses and in most cases will further increase the stresses.

As the result stands, the safety factor relating to maximum stress indicates failure at a value around 0.65.

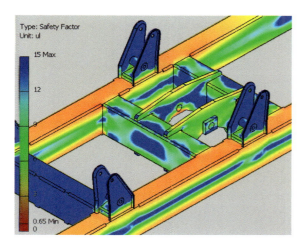

If the stress singularities are a very low percentage of the total joint area, local yielding can occur initially until the load is transmitted at lower stress by the full joint. As a rule of thumb, if such singularities result from static loading and are concentrated in small localized areas, then they can be ignored for the purposes of calculating the overall safety factor, for example. _Experience of the effect of such high stress points is needed to ensure that the correct interpretation is made of FEA results_. For example, dynamically loaded situations can have stress reversals; where these occur at welded joints, there is a high chance of fatigue failure occurring. In these situations, we can make use of the color bar to better understand the results, as suggested in the following steps:

22. Select **Von Mises Stress** > Select **Color Bar** > Unselect **Maximum** > Specify **355**MPa > Click **OK**

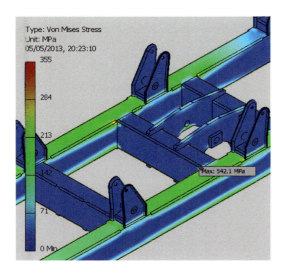

CHAPTER 6

DP5 - Assembly Analysis with built-in welds

 355MPa is the yield limit of the material used for the chassis.

 As the concentration of red color display is extremely low, and in this case stress reversals are unlikely, we can assume that safety factor of the design is above 1 for this case.

To determine what the safety factor actually is, however, and to illustrate zones of high stress requiring design changes, we can further manipulate the color bar. In the first instance, we will change the maximum value of the color bar again to 260MPa and then to 245MPa.

 Using **Contour Shading** rather than **Smooth Shading** to help isolate stress singularity stresses.

 Change the minimum value of the color bar in addition to the maximum value to help identify the areas of high stress.

 Change the number of legends to help identify the maximum value to be used for calculating the safety factor, despite having stress singularities present in the model

23. Select **Contour Shading** > Reselect **Color Bar** > Unselect **Maximum** > Specify **245** > Unselect **Minimum** > Specify **220** > Click **OK** > Look at **Front View**

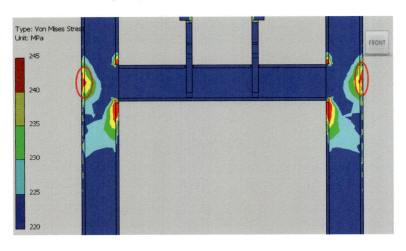

 As soon as we change the color bar maximum value to 245, we see the stresses above 240MPa are now appearing away from the welds and a picture of areas requiring redesign to optimize the chassis is becoming clear.

Now, by using the value of 240MPa, we can manipulate the color bar maximum value and number of legends to achieve the Von Mises plot shown on next page. Use your own value to calculate the safety factor, as mentioned above, as it may slightly differ.

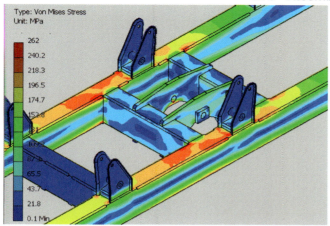

The above Von Mises plot confirms that the stress value around 240 starts to appear away from the weld areas due to bending. So, for the purposes of calculating safety factor, we will use the value of 240MPa (or use your calculated value).

$$Factor\ of\ Safety = \frac{355}{240} = 1.48$$

As the value is close to the design limit of 1.5, we will look at the planar stresses primarily occurring on the long channels, due to bending.

24. Double click **Stress YY**

25. Select **Color Bar** > Specify **300** for **Maximum Value** > Specify **-300** for **Minimum Value**> Increase the number of colors to **12** > Click **OK**

26. Select **Back View**

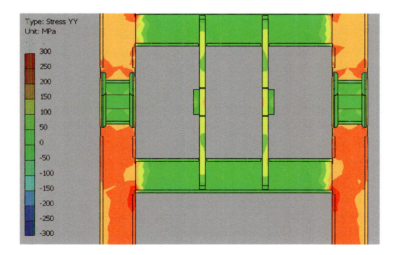

This displays tensile stresses along the long RHS member of the chassis. As indicated earlier, the highest stresses are located along the length of the chassis.

SECTION 2 - Stress Analysis Design Problems using Solid Elements

CHAPTER 6
DP5 - Assembly Analysis with built-in welds

27. Select **Front view** to display compressive stress

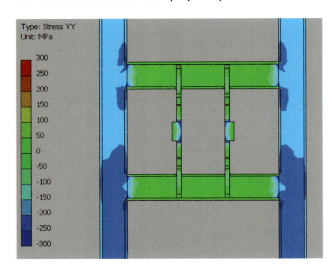

 The compressive and tensile stress display shows values above 250 MPa, which are relatively small in comparison to the width of the cross member. As loadings in this case are gradually applied and relatively infrequent, we will use this value to calculate safety factor.

$$Factor\ of\ Safety\ = \frac{355}{250} = 1.42$$

 This value is below the design limit.

28. Double Click **Displacement**

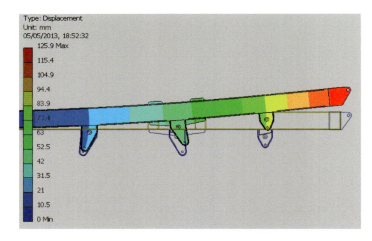

 The maximum displacement of the chassis is 125.9mm; this value is relatively high compared to the overall length of the chassis (approximately 7000 mm).

Basically, this analysis suggests that this design needs to be further stiffened to meet the design goal. In the next example, we will further idealize the chassis by removing the radii from the RHS channel. This will simply the model further but at the same time will further strengthen the chassis hence will not represent reality; however, it will give us an indication of whether chassis is more rigid.

Part 2 – Chassis design without welds and RHS member radii

At this stage, we will further idealize the model by removing the radii and inbuilt welds. This will help to remove stress singularities at the inbuilt welds. However it is important to note that this process will stiffen up the chassis, so care must be taken in interpreting results. The boundary conditions will remain unaltered and therefore there will be no need to apply them again.

Idealization

29. Right Click **Chassis-Analysis** > Select **Copy Simulation**

30. Expand **RL00007:1** component > Select the following components > Right Click > Select **Exclude from Simulation**

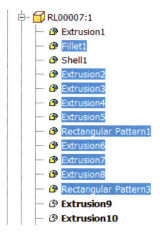

31. Expand **RL00013:1** component > Select the following components > Right Click > Select **Exclude from Simulation**

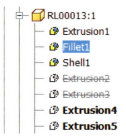

32. Expand **RL00008:2** component > Select the following components > Right Click > Select **Exclude from Simulation**

DP5 - Assembly Analysis with built-in welds

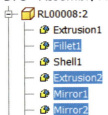

33. Expand **RL00024:1** component > Select the following components > Right Click > Select **Exclude from Simulation**

34. Expand **RL00034:1** component > Select the following components > Right Click > Select **Exclude from Simulation**

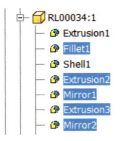

35. Right click **Contacts** > Select **Update Automatic Contacts** > Select **Mesh View**

 50780 Elements are generated. Elements generated

Rerun analysis and analyze

36. Select **Simulate** > Run **Analysis**

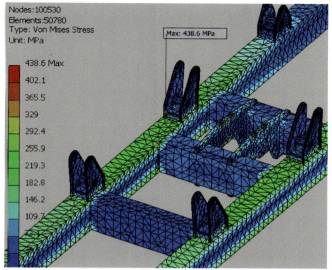

Maximum stress now occurs around the welds, and mounts, as before.

37. Double click **Stress YY** > Deselect **Maximum Value** > Select **Minimum Value**

38. Select **Color Bar** > > Specify **300** for **Maximum Value** > Specify **-300** for **Minimum Value**> Increase the number of colors to **12** > Click **OK** > Select **Front View**

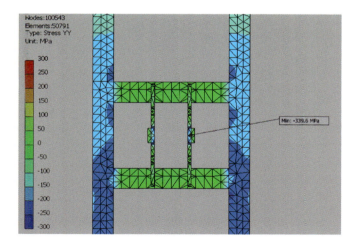

Maximum stress in the middle is compressive. As most components and welds in cases such as this usually fail due to tensile stress (and/or reversals) and not compressive stress, we will look at the tensile stress on the other side.

CHAPTER 6
DP5 - Assembly Analysis with built-in welds

39. Rotate the component to see the back view > Select **Maximum Value** > Deselect **Minimum Value**

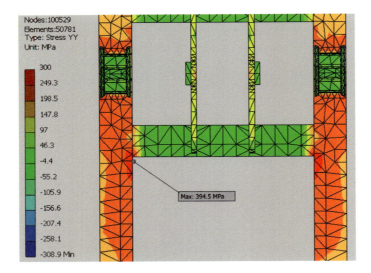

✏️ Apart from the stress singularities around the mounts, the maximum stress occurs on the main member, away from the cross member, unlike before.

✏️ There are no stress singularities between the cross member and the main member, as before

> **IMPORTANT** – To calculate factor of safety, use the color legend value below maximum value (or minimum value for compressive stress)

$$Tensile\ Factor\ of\ Safety = \frac{355}{250} = 1.42$$

40. Double click **Displacement;** the displacement value is around 119.2mm

Now, we will optimize the design in the next section to meet the design goals.

Optimization

Based on the previous analyzes of the chassis, the results indicate that the design does not meet the design criteria. To meet the design criteria, we have two options.

1. Increase the thickness of the RHS members; however, this approach is not cost- effective when compared to option 2 or if the component has already been manufactured.

2. Place a plate (suggested thickness ≥ 10mm) between the mounts and the RHS members for a distance that can be determined from the FEA results above(see picture on next page).

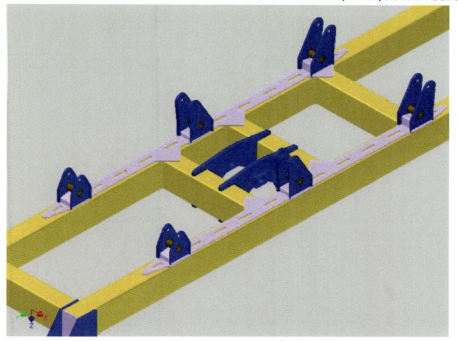

If the chassis design is not built, a combination of option 1 and 2 can be used to manufacture a more rigid chassis.

The following also illustrates another possible design for the new generation of trailer chassis

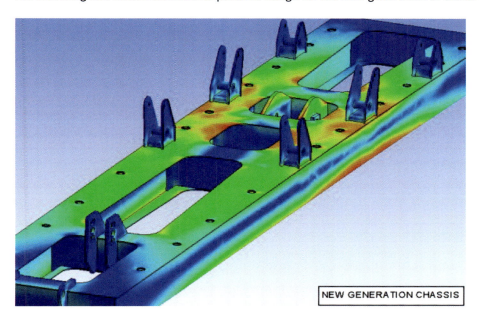

NEW GENERATION CHASSIS

In practice, <u>additional loading scenarios are analyzed</u>; for example, when the chassis has a torsional load applied down its length. In this case, stress reversals are often present that need to be taken into account when determining the final design of reinforcements to be made.

SECTION 2 - Stress Analysis Design Problems using Solid Elements

Section 3 - STRESS ANALYSIS *Design Problems* using THIN ELEMENTS

DP6 – Wind Load analysis

Structural Integrity of Traffic Sign Posts
(Design Problem Courtesy of VMS Ltd)

Key features and workflows introduced in this design problem

	Key Features/Workflows
1	Effective use of multi-bodies with respect to different midsurface thicknesses
2	Creating Surfaces using Midsurface command
3	Creating Surfaces using Offset command
4	Wind speed load converted to force

Introduction

Variable Message Signs Limited (VMS) has been a market leader for a quarter of a century and supplied thousands of messaging signs and traffic management systems. VMS products fall into two main categories: Road - with a product range covering applications in the highways, urban, and traffic management equipment sectors, and Rail, where their new super lightweight range of rail LED trackside signals and LED long-distance signals are breaking the mould in this sector.

SECTION 3 - Stress Analysis Design Problems using Thin Elements

CHAPTER 7

DP6 - Wind Load Analysis

The main requirements of this design problem are to determine:

1. Maximum stress in the structure.
2. Maximum displacement of the structure
3. Minimum safety factor.

In addition to the above requirements, the design criteria to be used for this design problem are:

- The material to be used is mild steel.
- Wind speeds to be taken as 25mph and 50 mph
- Weight of Display panel is 60Kg.

Workflow of Design Problem 6

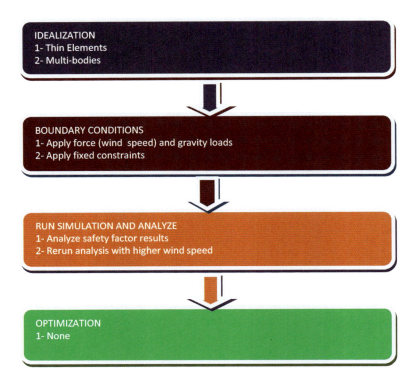

IDEALIZATION
1- Thin Elements
2- Multi-bodies

BOUNDARY CONDITIONS
1- Apply force (wind speed) and gravity loads
2- Apply fixed constraints

RUN SIMULATION AND ANALYZE
1- Analyze safety factor results
2- Rerun analysis with higher wind speed

OPTIMIZATION
1- None

Idealization

As Inventor Simulation only creates midsurfaces for a single thickness component, we are going to make use of multibodies, with different thicknesses, within a single component, as illustrated below. This way Inventor Simulation will select all features of the single component for potential midsurface creation as demonstrated in this design problem. Further to simplify the analysis process for this example; the display, fixtures and fittings and the concrete base, will be excluded from the simulation. This simplification and idealization are saved as different level of details within the assembly environment and will be used in the analysis.

1. Open *SignPost*.iam

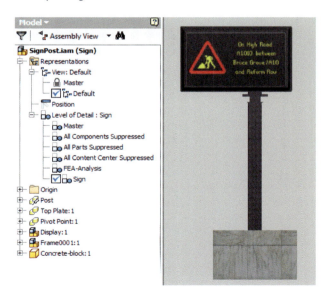

2. Activate **FEA-Analysis** Level of Detail

This will suppress the sign and concrete block for the purposes of analysis

3. Select **Environments** tab > Select **Stress Analysis**

4. Select **Create Simulation** > Specify **Signpost** for **Name** > Click **OK**

 Create midsurfaces before applying constraints and loads as these will be lost if applied on component faces.

5. Select **Find Thin Bodies** > Click **OK** in the prompt dialogue box

6. Select other components, except frame behind panel > Expand **Prompts** button > Select **Do not show this message again this session** > Click **OK** > Continue selecting the rest of the component > Click **OK,** once selected all.

 If you miss a component just select the midsurface button and continue selecting rest of components

 You cannot use **Find Thin Bodies** command twice

As the posts of made up of different thicknesses we have made use of multibodies as this results in different midsurface thicknesses as illustrated below. The alternative would have been to create the post as an assembly comprised of different components

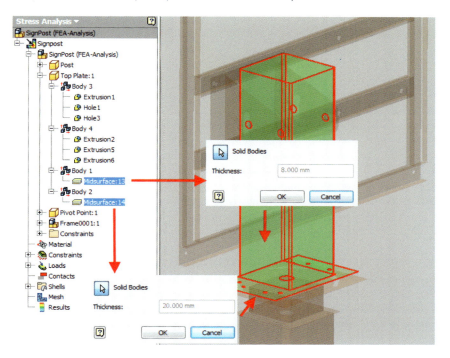

Autodesk Simulation will create a single midsurface with average thickness for a part with multiple thicknesses if used without multibodies.

The frames supporting the LED panel comprise of tapered structures, meaning that the structures will result in multiple disconnected surfaces as shown below

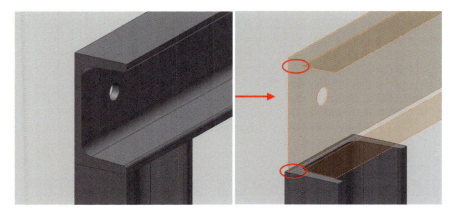

CHAPTER 7
DP6 - Wind Load Analysis
This can be avoided by using offset surfaces command as illustrated below

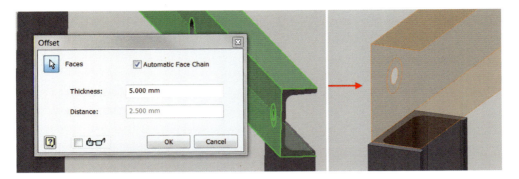

The Thickness parameter is an estimate of the channel as the thicknesses varies from 5 to 8mm. The value chosen illustrates worst case scenario. The benefit of this method is that all surfaces are connected. In the following steps the frames will be converted to surfaces using the offset surface command.

 By using Offset command you can perform different simulations by altering the thickness parameters to see the effect on the structure

7. Select the **Offset** command from the **Prepare** panel > Select the faces of the frame as shown > Specify **5**mm for Thickness > Click **OK**

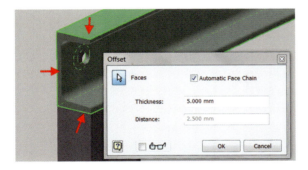

8. Repeat Step 7 for all the frames selecting all external faces

SECTION 3 - Stress Analysis Design Problems using Thin Elements

Boundary conditions

In the following steps we will apply constraints and loads.

9. Select **Fixed Constraint** > Select the four faces as shown > Click **OK**

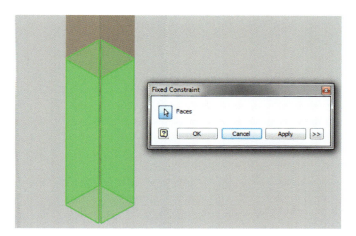

✏️ The faces have been already split in the part environment. These faces are normally restrained by the concrete base, excluded from this analysis.

In the next steps we need to apply wind speed exerted directly on LED Display (excluded from this analysis). Here we have two overcome two issues first too convert wind speed into force as we cannot apply wind speed in Inventor Simulation 2013. Secondly we need to apply this force on the panel at the location where the Display is connected to the frame via bushings. As we are not including bushing in the analysis we will apply the loads on the edge of the four hole locations, were the bushing are located.

For the purposes of calculating force from a given wind speed we will use the following generic formula (googled on the world wide web)

$$Force\ F = A\ x\ P\ x\ Cd\ \ and\ P = 0.12257\ x\ V^2$$

Where:

F is force in Newtons (N)

A is the cross section of the LED display panel in Meters (approx 2m^2)

P is the pressure in Pascals (N/m)

V is the wind speed in (Mph)

Cd is the drag coefficient (2 to be used for rectangular flat areas)

For a wind speed of 25mph we get the total force to be

CHAPTER 7
DP6 - Wind Load Analysis

$$P = 0.12257 \times 25^2 = 76.6$$

$$Force \; F = 2 \times 76.6 \times 2 = 306N$$

10. Select **Force** and specify **306**N > Select the circular face as shown below

11. Select the other three circular faces > Specify **25**mph for **Name** > Select front face of top frame for **Direction** of load > Click **Apply**

Now we are going to account for the 60Kg weight of the display panel. This converted to force will be approximately 600N

12. Specify **600**N > Select the same hole circular faces again > Specify **Weight of panel** for **Name** > Select edge of side frame for **Direction** of load > Flip **Direction** > Change color of Load to **red** > Click **OK**

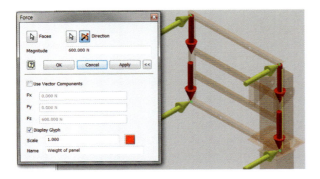

SECTION 3 - Stress Analysis Design Problems using Thin Elements

13. Select **Automatic Contacts**

14. Select **Mesh Settings** > Specify **0.04** for **Average Element Size in Shells** > Click **OK**

15. Select **Mesh View**

A total of 25,116 elements will be created, value may differ slightly.

Run simulation and analyze

16. Select **Simulate** > Run **Analysis**

17. Select **Undeformed** for **Displacement Display** > Deselect **Boundary Conditions** > Deselect **Mesh View** > Select **Maximum Value**

18. Select **Contour Shading** > Select **Color Bar Settings** > Unselect **Maximum** > Specify **6** > Click **OK**

Value may differ slightly slightly for stress and displacement

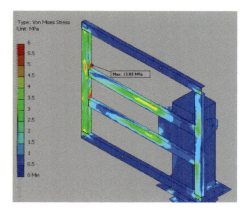

19. Select **Displacement**

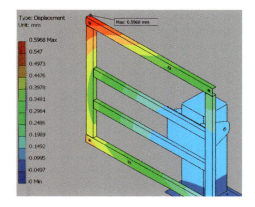

Maximum value is 0.5968. Now we are going to copy the simulation and reanalyze structure for wind speed of 50mph

20. Right Click **Signpost** > Select **Copy Simulation**

21. Right Click **Contacts** > Select **Update Automatic Contacts**

22. Right Click 25mph Load > Select **Edit Force Load** > Specify **1225.7**N > Specify **50**mph for **Name** > Click **OK**

$$P = 0.12257 \; x \; 50^2 = 306.425$$

$$Force \; F = 2 \; x \; 306.425 \; x \; 2 \; = \; 1225.7N$$

23. Select **Simulate** > Run **Analysis**

24. Select **Displacement**

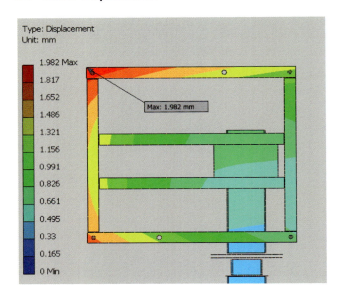

The displacement value has more than doubled which will also result in higher stresses , which need to be investigated.

25. Close File

DP7 – Fabrication Analysis

Structural Integrity of Container
(Design Problem Courtesy of Croft Associates Ltd)

Key features and workflows introduced in this design problem

	Key Features/Workflows
1	Creating Surfaces using Midsurface command
2	Creating Surfaces using Offset command
3	Combined thin and solid elements

Introduction

Croft Associates Limited specializes in all aspects of the packaging and transport of radioactive materials. Since establishment in 1980, the company has developed an extensive range of packaging designs for standard products, and for customers' individual requirements.

CHAPTER 8
DP7 - Fabrication Analysis

Croft customers are often governmental organizations and private companies in the nuclear materials and waste industries. In addition, research reactors, hospitals and medical equipment suppliers also use the company products to transport radioactive materials for recovery, verification, testing, compliance assurance and medical applications.

The main requirements of this design problem are to determine:

1. Maximum stress within the base structure of the container assembly
2. Maximum displacement under the loads specified under the various regulatory specifications pertaining to hazardous material transport

In addition to the main requirements, the design criteria to be used for this design problem are:

- The material to be used is Steel, High Strength Low Alloy
- The maximum allowable vertical permanent displacement of 6mm, ie. the floor cannot be allowed to (displace) below the main supporting components (the four corner fittings which interface with corresponding components in, for example, a nine high stack of equivalent containers). The floor may displace further than 6mm , but must recover to an extent that any permanent set allows sufficient clearance for the container to be stored in a stacking arrangement.
- The maximum operational stress not to exceed 2/3rd of material yield limit.

Workflow of Design Problem 7

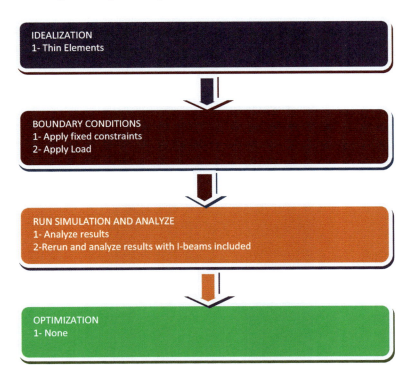

IDEALIZATION
1- Thin Elements

BOUNDARY CONDITIONS
1- Apply fixed constraints
2- Apply Load

RUN SIMULATION AND ANALYZE
1- Analyze results
2-Rerun and analyze results with I-beams included

OPTIMIZATION
1- None

Idealization

In this example we going to only consider the base of the component as the main structural item of the container as this will carry the bulk of the load. Although the rest of the components will provide some structural support it is assumed it will minimal and will be neglected for the purposes of this design problem. In reality the I-Beams will be actually fixed to the base of the components before container is loaded. In this example we will consider the effect of I-Beams having on the overall structural integrity of the base when loaded. Further, to simplify the modeling process for this example, all welds and the fixture and fittings of the base plate will be excluded from the simulation. This simplification and idealization are saved as different level of details within the assembly environment and will be used in the analysis.

1. Open *Container*.iam

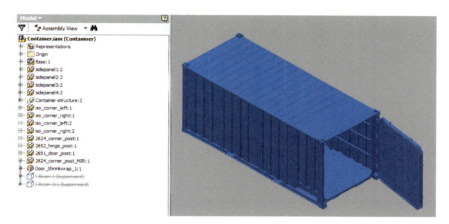

2. Activate **FEA** Level of Detail

This level of detail suppresses the side and top panels, including door and fittings. In additional all fixture and fitting on the base panel are also suppressed.

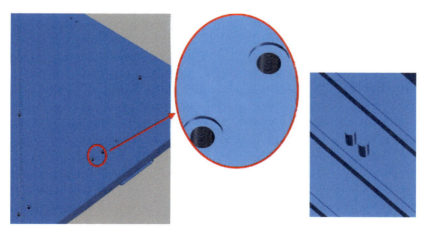

CHAPTER 8
DP7 - Fabrication Analysis
Boundary conditions

3. Select **Environments** tab > Select **Stress Analysis**

4. Select **Create Simulation** > Specify **Base** for **Name** > Click **OK**

You can further simplify by excluding the holes from the analysis. Remember as theses holes were referenced in some assembly constraints using exclude from simulation feature will not work. One of the workarounds will be to suppress the features within assembly environment and then accept warnings referring to loss of assembly constraints reference. In this example we will not suppress the holes.

5. Select **Fixed Constraint** > Select bottom face of corner component as shown

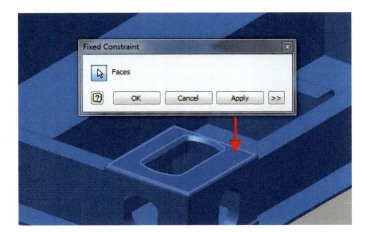

📝 If you are going to use thin elements then suggest applying constraints after creating midsurfaces as the face selected for constraints (on solid) will be lost. Here we are going to use the corner as solid hence makes no difference as the face will be retained in the analysis.

6. Now select the faces of the other three corners > Click **OK**

In the next steps we are going to apply loads to the base. In reality there will be a pair of I-beams fixed to base, at the location of the holes. In this example we want to see the affect of adding the I-beams will have on the overall stiffness of the base when loaded. The top face of base plate component has faces already split in the part environment, enabling us to select them to apply loads, otherwise the load will have to be applied on whole face which can produce different results.

7. Select **Force** and specify **100,000**N > Select the two split faces > Specify **Total Load** for **Name** > Click **OK**

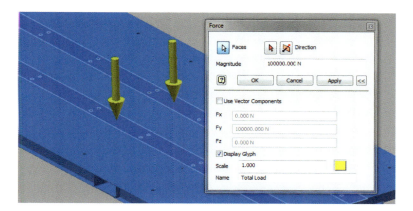

Do not select Automatic Contacts before creating midsurfaces to be used for thin elements, as the contacts produced will between solid components and not the midsurfaces.

8. Select **Find Thin Bodies** > Click **OK** in the prompt dialogue box

As there are a lot of bodies to be converted we will stop and see which one's need converting

None converted components will not be shown as transparent surfaces

9. Click **OK**

As we had applied the loads on the base plate we have lost the load associativity, as the original face does not exist. Also as we have used the midsurface option the split faces have been merged with the rest of the plate faces. The workaround to this is to delete the midsurface created and to use offset command instead. Also worth mentioning, as indicated previously, is to create surfaces first and then apply boundary conditions on the newly created surfaces.

10. Expand **Shells** folder > Then expand **Base:1::3123_floor_panel:1** folder > Right Click Midsurface:22 > Select **Delete**

11. Select **Offset** command from **Prepare** panel > Specify **6**mm for **Thickness** > Select one of the faces of the base panel component > Click **OK**

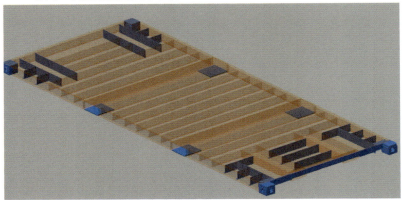

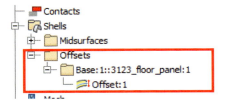 A separate folder will be created for surfaces created by using Offset command

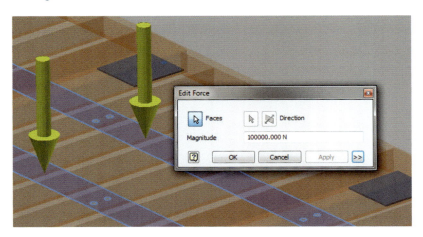

12. Right Click **Total Load** > Select **Edit Force Load** > Select the two split faces again

13. Click **OK**

14. Select **Midsurface** command from **Prepare** panel > Select all the remaining components (except corner block and plates) > Click **OK** (to finish command)

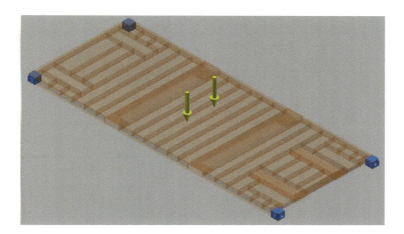

💡 You can press Ok anytime and if any components are left over (still blue) you can select the Midsurface command again. Sometimes it's good practice to do this especially when there are too many components to be converted manually to midsurfaces

15. Select **Mesh Settings** > Unselect **Use part based measure for Assembly mesh** > Click **OK**

16. Select **Mesh View**

A total of 18671 elements will be created, value may differ slightly.

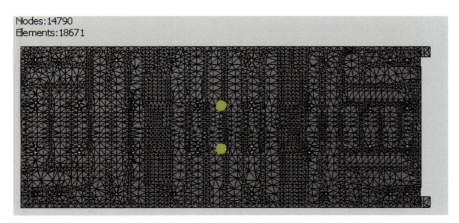

📝 Leaving Use part based measure for Assembly would have resulted in excess of 100,000 elements.

CHAPTER 8
DP7 - Fabrication Analysis
Run simulation and analyze

17. Select **Simulate**

A warning will appear saying that materials have not been defined correctly

18. Select **Cancel** > Select **Assign** > Select first row of unassigned material in **Override Material** column > Keeping the **shift key pressed** select the last row > Select **Steel, High Strength Low Alloy** > Click **OK**

All component will now have a new assigned material as shown below

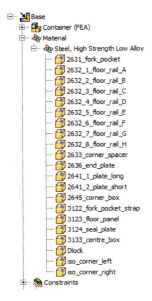

19. Select **Simulate** > Run **Analysis**

20. Select **Undeformed** for **Displacement Display** > Select **Contour Shading** > Select **Show Max value** in **Display** > Select **Color Bar Settings** > Unselect **Maximum** > Specify **200** > Click **OK**

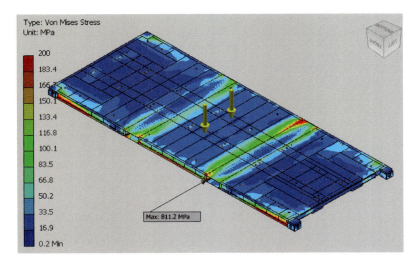

SECTION 3 - Stress Analysis Design Problems using Thin Elements

21. Select **Displacement**

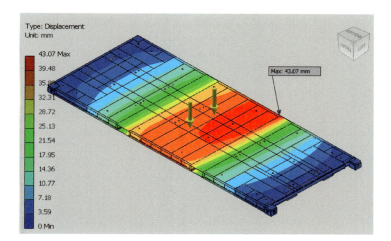

The maximum displacement of 43.07mm is too high. Due to this high deflection we get high working stresses which is well above the yield limit of the material, which is 275MPa. Now we will see the affect of adding two I-Beams on the base.

22. Right Click **Base** > Select **Copy Simulation**

23. Right Click **Base:1** > Select **Edit Simulation Properties** > Select **Model State** > Change **Level of Detail** from **FEA** to **FEA With I-Beams** > Click **OK**

24. Select **Midsurface** command > Select both I-Beams > Click **OK**

25. Now Right Click **Contacts** > Select **Update Automatic Contacts**

26. Right Click **Total Load** > Select **Edit Force Load** > Keeping the **Shift Key** pressed select the split surfaces used to define the original load (this will deselect the faces) > Select the top surfaces of each I-Beam.

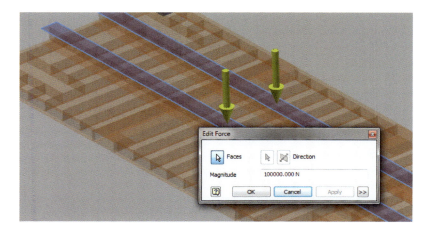

27. Click **OK**

28. Select **Mesh View** > Select **Simulate** > Select **Run**

29. Unselect **Mesh View** > Select **Color Bar Settings** > Unselect **Maximum** > Specify **200** > Click **OK**

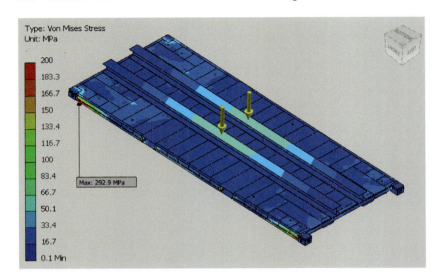

The maximum stress is now reduced to 292.9MPa which is higher than 2/3rd of chosen material. In reality these highly stressed components normally use a different grade of steel with a higher yield limit.

30. Select **Displacement**

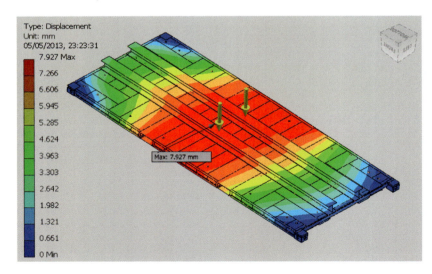

The maximum displacement has significantly reduced to 7.927mm.

31. Close File

DP8 – Sheet Metal Analysis

Structural Validation of Hopper
(Design Problem Courtesy of Simba Great Plains Ltd)

Key features and workflows introduced in this design problem

	Key Features/Workflows
1	Symmetry conditions using thin elements
2	Displaying symmetrical results using ground plane and reflections

Introduction

On 30th April 2010, Simba International Limited was acquired by Great Plains Mfg., Inc, based in Salina, Kansas, USA bringing together the product innovation, expertise, experience and knowledge cf two of the world's leading brands in tillage equipment. Backed by the vast resources of North America's largest non-tractor, privately owned agricultural implement manufacturing company, the future for Simba, now rebranded Simba Great Plains, looks brighter than ever

Simba Great Plains products mainly cater for the agricultural industry and a typical product is a seed hopper as illustrated in the above image.

The main requirements of this design problem are to determine:

CHAPTER 9
DP8 - Sheet Metal Analysis

1. Whether the seed hopper can withstand a load of 3000 Kg
2. Maximum Stress and Displacement.

In addition to the above requirements, the design criteria to be used for this design problem are:

- The material to be used is mild steel.
- Minimum factor of safety required is 2.

Workflow of Design Problem 8

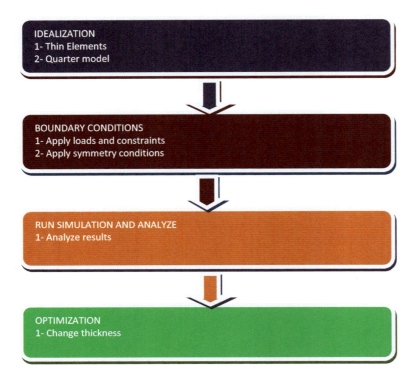

Idealization

In this design problem due to the symmetrical loading and geometry of the hopper we are going to analyze a quarter of the model and suppress all the non structural components including lid and all fasteners. Again all of this information is saved as a level of detail and an extrusion within assembly environment used to split the assembly into a quarter assembly.

1. Open *Hopper*.iam

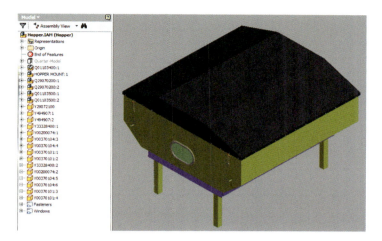

2. Activate **Hopper-Analysis** > Move **End of Features** below **Quarter-Model** feature

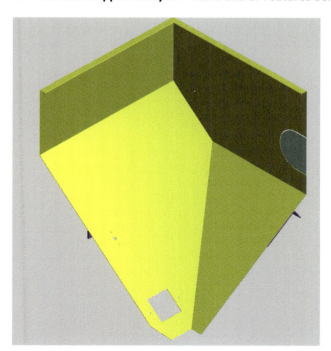

Boundary conditions

3. Select **Environments** tab > Select **Stress Analysis**

4. Select **Create Simulation** > Specify **Quarter-Model** for **Name**

5. Change Contacts Tolerance to **1**mm > Click **OK**

6. Select **Find Thin Bodies** > Click **OK** > Select rest of components > Click **OK,** once selected all components.

7. Select **Fixed Constraint** > Select the four bottom edges of the hopper leg as shown > Click **OK**

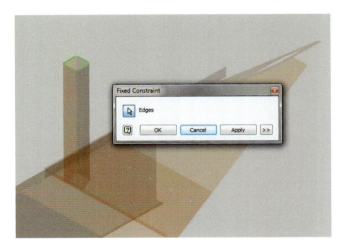

8. Select **Frictionless Constraint** > Select all the edges created as a result of using the split command as shown > Specify **Symmetry** for **Name** > Click **OK**

SECTION 3 - Stress Analysis Design Problems using Thin Elements

9.   Select **Force** and specify **7500**N > Select the two sloping surfaces as shown below > Specify **Weight** for **Name** > Select the edge of the hopper, as shown, for **Direction** of load > Click **OK**

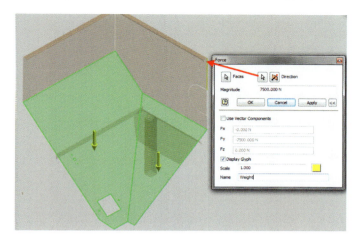

As we are analyzing a quarter model we will divide total load of 3 tonnes (30,000N) by 4 giving 7500N

10. Select **Automatic Contacts**

A total of 35 contacts will be created. We will now create contacts manually for windows and mount frame in the following steps

11. **Select Manual Contact** > Select two edges as shown > Click **Apply**

12. Select the next two edges as shown > Click **Apply**

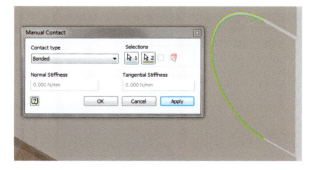

SECTION 3 - Stress Analysis Design Problems using Thin Elements

13. Select the final two edges as shown > Click **Apply**

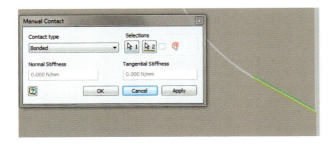

14. Now select the surface and edge as shown > Click **OK**

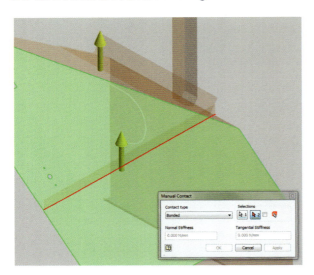

15. Select **Mesh View**

A total of 17443 elements will be created, value may differ slightly.

Run simulation and analyze

16. Select **Simulate** > Run **Analysis**

17. Select **1st Principal Stress** >Select **Mesh View** > Select **Undeformed** for **Displacement Display** > Deselect **Boundary Conditions**

18. Select **Contour Shading** > Select **Show Max value** in **Display** > Select **Color Bar Settings >** Unselect **Maximum >** Specify **300 >** Click **OK**

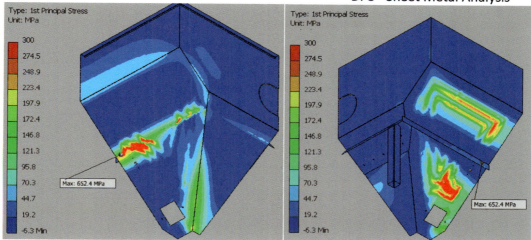

The actual value of the stresses may differ, what's more important at this stage is they are high. The 1st Principal Stress shows maximum tensile stresses in the hopper. The maximum stress inside the hopper is around the mount which is restraining the displacement. The stresses at the back of the hopper are due to stretching of the metal due to excessive displacement.

19. Select **Displacement** and then **Safety Factor**

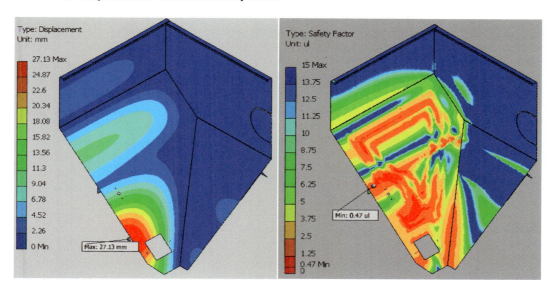

By analyzing the safety factor we can see the minimum value is below 1. This may well be due to stress singularities. However if we are not comfortable we could perform another analysis with a different material with a higher yield limit. Or perhaps we could alter the design to reduce maximum stress. In the following steps we are going to increase the thickness of the hopper body from 2 to 3 mm

20. Finish **Stress Analysis**

CHAPTER 9

DP8 - Sheet Metal Analysis

21. Change thickness of the following components to **3**mm . Accept warning as it relates to constraints

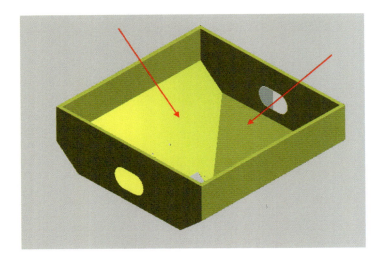

💡An alternative way to experiment with different thin element thicknesses is to use Offset command and specify different thickness values.

22. Select **Environments** tab > Select **Stress Analysis**

23. Right click **Contacts** > Select **Update Automatic Contacts**

24. Right click **Mesh** > Select **Update Mesh**

25. Select **Simulate** > Run **Analysis** > Select **1st Principal Stress** > Deselect **Maximum Value**

26. Unselect **Mesh View** > Select **Color Bar** > Specify **150** for **Maximum value** > Click **OK**

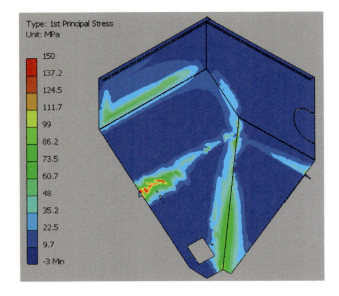

SECTION 3 - Stress Analysis Design Problems using Thin Elements

27. Select **Safety Factor** > Deselect **Maximum Value**

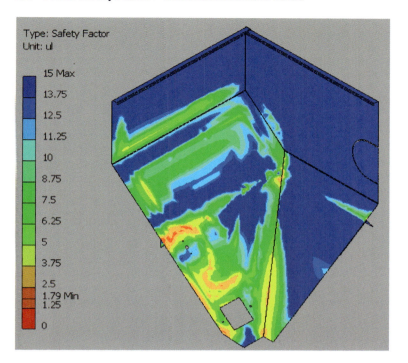

By changing the thickness the safety factor has increased to above 1.

Make use of ground plane and 100% reflection to display symmetrical results

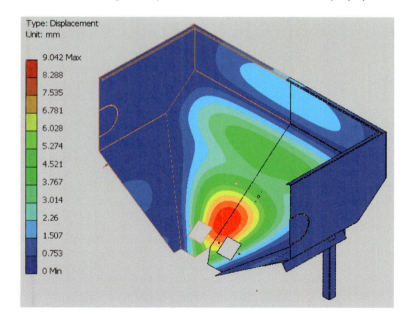

28. Close File

DP9 – 20g Acceleration

Structural Integrity of Police Van Cell
(Design Problem Courtesy of James Alpe Ltd)

Key features and workflows introduced in this design problem

	Key Features/Workflows
1	Idealization including Shrinkwrap with Multibodies
2	Manual Contacts
3	Acceleration Loads

Introduction

James Alpe Vehicle Conversions, based in Clitheroe UK, specialise in bespoke conversions for both the public and private sectors. They have built up a strong reputation as one of the country's leading vehicle conversions specialists carrying out work for many Police Forces, Ambulance Trusts, the MOD, Her Majesty's Prison Service, Schools, local councils, and many private sector organisations. From Police cell vans to dog vans from horse boxes to exhibition trailers.

James Alpe Vehicle Conversions offer a comprehensive range of solutions for all commercial and specialist vehicle users. Their in-house team of coachbuilders, fabricators, electricians and technicians can fulfill almost any brief. Whether it is a mass fleet vehicle production or a bespoke one-off specialist conversion we can meet the unique requirements of our broad customer base.

SECTION 3 - Stress Analysis Design Problems using Thin Elements

CHAPTER 10
DP9 - 20g Acceleration

On occasions James Alpe subcontracts out expensive and timely physical tests of their products, in this case a police van cell. The test is basically causing a frontal crash of a police van into a brick wall at 30mph, generating around 20g accelerations. Although the actual test will have a dummy passenger in the cell, in this example we will simulate a police van cell crashing at 30mph without any occupants. The main emphasis of this example will be around preparing the model for simulation as this is a typical example of complex fabrication which is to detailed for analysis. This problem presents a common dilemma of whether to rebuilt a model again for analysis purposes or try to simplify the CAD model. In this example the latter approach is taken.

Workflow of Design Problem 9

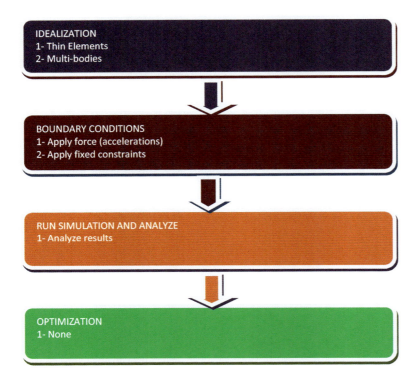

IDEALIZATION
1- Thin Elements
2- Multi-bodies

BOUNDARY CONDITIONS
1- Apply force (accelerations)
2- Apply fixed constraints

RUN SIMULATION AND ANALYZE
1- Analyze results

OPTIMIZATION
1- None

Idealization

The model to be used for this design problem is too detailed for stress analysis environment. The model needs to be significantly simplified. At this stage we have two options either create a new model for analysis purposes or simplify original model, both methods will require time. The benefit of the latter method is the link between design and analysis will be maintained thus making it easier for reanalysis, once a design change has been made. In most cases the designer and analyst will be the same person hence making sense to simplify the model. The designer has various options to simplify including;

1. Level of Details
2. Shrinkwrap Substitute
3. Defeaturing
4. Shrinkwrap
5. Fusion

I will go through each option explaining the pro's and con's.

Level of Details: This is fastest and easiest method to suppress non-structural components. As soon as the non-structural components are suppressed inventor will create a new level of detail. Once this new level of detail is saved the designer can switch between level of details by simply clicking on the desired level of detail. This method does not work at the feature level.

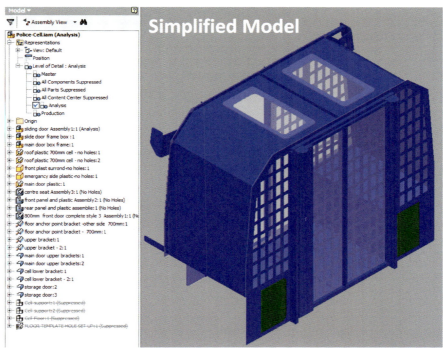

Shrinkwrap Substitute: This method works just like a level of detail with the added benefit of being able to simplify geometry mainly by suppressing unwanted holes.

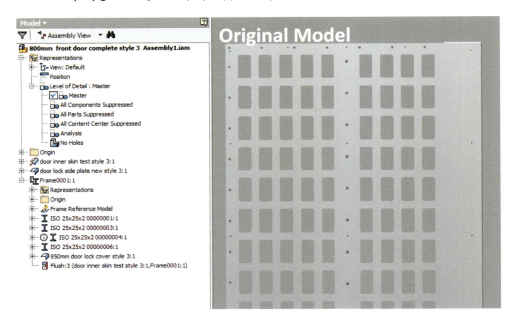

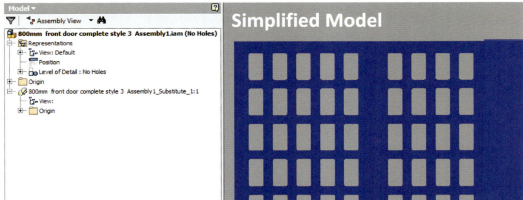

Defeaturing: This method allows to simplify components by suppressing features of parts. The main disadvantage of this method is that it will change the component and taking these changes through to the drawings. This method will only work if you make a copy of the original and then defeature

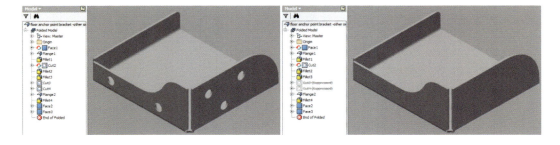

Shrinkwrap: This method is similar to Shrinkwrap Substitute with the main difference that the simplified model is saved as a separate file and not as a level of detail. This method in combination with defeaturing will prove to be useful if the model is complex and requires a lot of defeaturing. To maintain the link the simplified model will have to be placed in the original assembly over the original model. Then using level of details suppress and unsuppress the desired component. Yes I know it sounds tedious but the other option is to create a new model, which can be more tedious.

Fusion: This is by far the best method to simplify complex geometry without affecting the original model, as the simplified model is saved as a fusion drawing. Fusion also offers the ability to find and suppress features including holes, fillets, chamfers, boss and much more.

Suggested Idealization Workflow for Detailed Fabrications

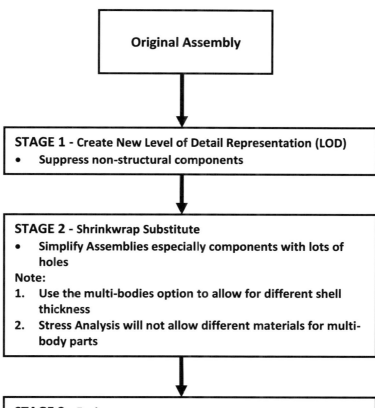

Original Assembly

STAGE 1 - Create New Level of Detail Representation (LOD)
- Suppress non-structural components

STAGE 2 - Shrinkwrap Substitute
- Simplify Assemblies especially components with lots of holes

Note:
1. Use the multi-bodies option to allow for different shell thickness
2. Stress Analysis will not allow different materials for multi-body parts

STAGE 3 - Fusion
- Defeature and simplify components instead of feature suppression using Fusion

Note:
1. You will need to place the simplified component in the original assembly. I suggest place over original component and use LOD to manage component suppression
2. If there are too many parts suggest copy the assembly and replace with simplified components

CHAPTER 10

DP9 - 20g Acceleration

1. Open *Police-Cell.*iam

This assembly has already been through the simplification process based on the suggested workflow.

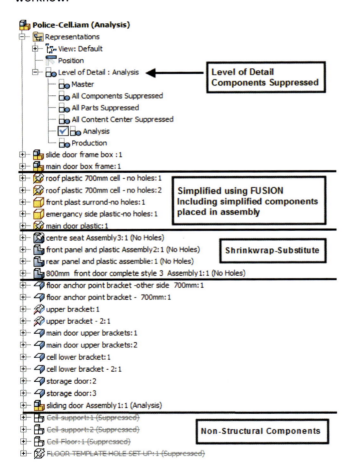

Boundary conditions

2.   Select **Environments** tab > Select **Stress Analysis**

3.   Select **Create Simulation** > Specify **20**g **Acceleration** for **Name** > Click **OK**

📝 Create midsurfaces before applying constraints and loads as these will be lost if applied on component faces.

4.   Select **Midsurface** from the **Prepare** panel > Select all components

💡 If you miss a component just select the midsurface button and continue selecting rest of components as they will be visible

📝 You cannot use **Find Thin Bodies** command twice

💡 You can always select Midsurface again if you miss a component, as it will be visible

5.   Select **Fixed Constraint** > Select the nine faces as shown below > Click **OK**

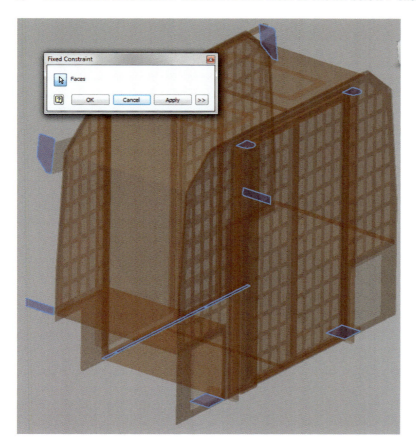

CHAPTER 10
DP9 - 20g Acceleration

6. Select **Body Loads** from the **Load** panel > Activate **Enable Linear Acceleration** > Activate **Use Vector Components** > Specify **9810*20** in the Z Vector Component magnitude field > Click **OK**

7. Select **Automatic Contacts.** Note this can take several minutes

Approximately 220 contacts will be created. As there are too many contacts it is tedious to go through all to make sure surfaces are in contact. I suggest not to examine contacts at this stage but only after you select Simulate as the software will detect any components that are not in contact. It is at this stage you can quickly create contacts between components as specified by the software.

However it is important to note as the original model contains fillets/radii this will result in adjacent surfaces having to many contacts. In the example below one contact between surfaces would have sufficed. As it tedious to go through all contacts. I suggest to only suppress contacts in the areas resulting in high stresses (probably due to stress singularities)

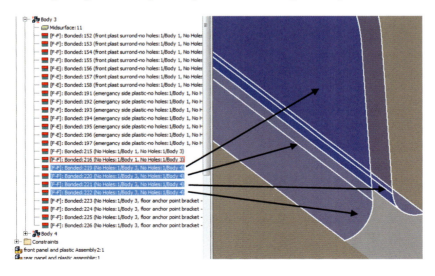

SECTION 3 - Stress Analysis Design Problems using Thin Elements

8. Select **Mesh Settings** > Specify **0.1** for **Average Element Size in Shells** > Specify **0.5** for **Minimum Element Size** > Unselect **Use part based measured for Assembly Mesh** > Click **OK**

Specifying a higher value for Minimum Element Size will help to reduce the number of elements generated.

9. Select **Mesh View**

Run simulation and analyze

10. Select **Simulate**

The following error and warning will appear in the Simulate dialogue box as shown > Click **Cancel**

The error is due to the fact the assemblies which were shrink-wrapped were not assigned materials with the assembly environment. Therefore we will assign materials within the Stress Analysis environment.

The warning suggests there are no contacts between some components as they have gaps in excess of the specified simulation contact settings. These gaps are primarily down to supressing components that were placed instead of the gaps. To remove the warnings we will create manual contacts.

11. Select **Assign** from the **Materials** panel > Select all four subassemblies as shown using left mouse button and shift key > Select **Steel Mild** from the Override Material column > Click **OK**

CHAPTER 10

DP9 - 20g Acceleration

12. Select **Manual Contact** from the **Contacts** manual

13. Select the two faces of the bracket and the front panel as shown > Click **Apply**

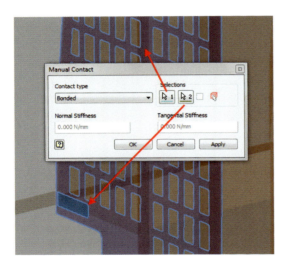

14. Now repeat for the bracket on the other side > Click **Apply**

15. Select the face of the back door and support as shown > Click **Apply**

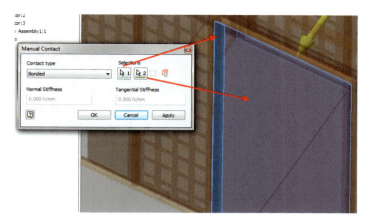

16. Now repeat for the other side of the door > Click **Apply**

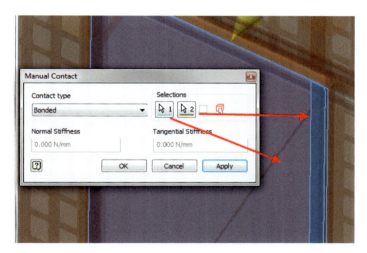

17. Select the face of the back door and support as shown > Click **Apply**

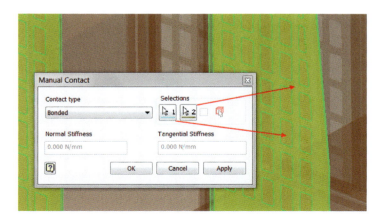

18. Now repeat for the other side of the cell, as shown below > Click **OK**

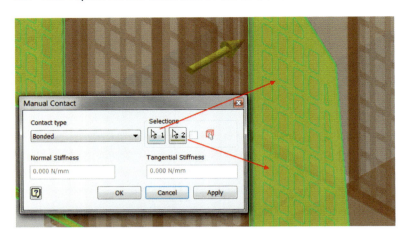

19. Select **Simulate** > Select Run **Analysis**

20. Select **Displacement** > Select **Adjusted x 1** for **Adjustment Scale**

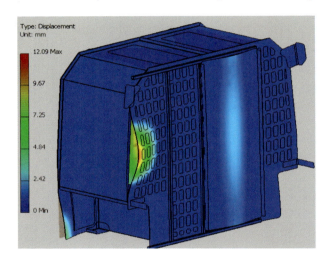

We can see from the image above there is a missing contact. For complex fabrications this is one of the ways to check for any missing contacts between parts alternatively you can further simply the model by removing radii, cutouts and other sheet metal features. In this example we create another manual contact

21. Select **Manual Contact** > Select following components > Click **OK**

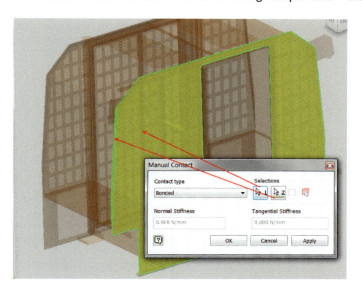

22. Select **Simulate** > Run **Analysis**

23. Select **Displacement** Results

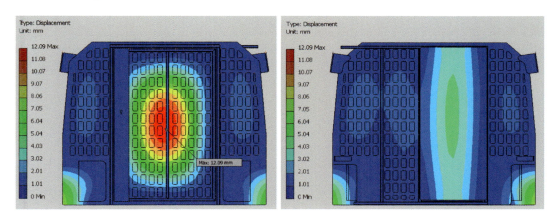

Ycu can further investigate the stress and safety factor results. of the model.

24. Close File

CHAPTER 10
DP9 - 20g Acceleration

Section 4 -
STRESS ANALYSIS
Design Problems
using MOTION LOADS
from Dynamic Simulation

NB: Dynamic Simulation not covered in this book

DP10 – Motion Load Transfer Analysis

Structural Validation of Mounting Lugs

(Design Problem Courtesy of In-CAD Services Ltd)

Key features and workflows introduced in this design problem

	Key Features/Workflows
1	Motion loads
2	Manipulating constraints - to remove peak stresses
2	Optimization

Introduction

This design problem will look at the effective use of Dynamic Simulation to validate the structural integrity of the mounting lugs. The force will be exported from the simulation study and will be directly used in the Stress analysis environment removing the need to apply loads and restraints.

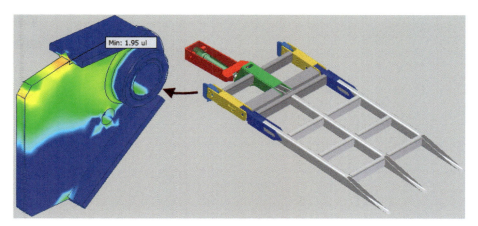

The main requirements of this design problem are to determine:

1. Maximum stress in the mounting lugs when the ramp is fully loaded.
2. Factor of safety - for example, the fatigue life could be predicted.

In addition to the above requirements, the design criteria to be used for this design problem are:

- The material to be used is mild steel.
- The factor of safety required is 2.
- Impact loading will not be taken into account.

SECTION 4 - Stress Analysis Design Problems using Motion Loads from Dynamic Simulation

Workflow of Design Problem 10

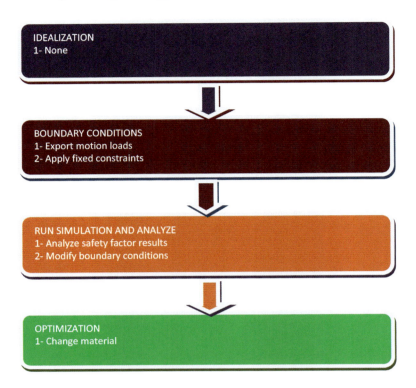

Idealization

The geometry of the model to be analyzed is simple and therefore is no need to further simplify. However, the loads in this example will be transferred from the Dynamic Simulation environment.

1. Open *Ramp-Open*.iam

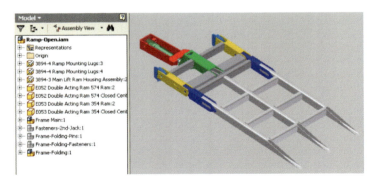

2. Select **Environments** tab > Select **Dynamic Simulation**

Boundary conditions

3.   Play **Simulation >** Select **Yes** to accept warning > Select **Output Grapher**

4.   Right Click Force (Spherical:3) column > Select **Search Max**

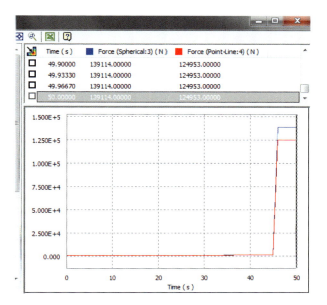

The maximum force for Force (Spherical:3) joint is 139114N and it's the same between 46 and 50 seconds . We will export this force to the Stress Analysis environment.

Export motion loads

5.   Tick in the **Export to FEA** column at 50 seconds to export loads at this time frame

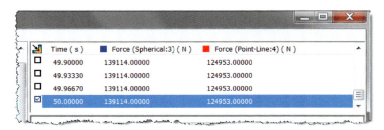

This time step is now added. Note that any time step between 46 and 50 can be used.

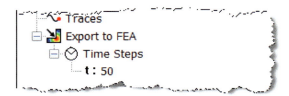

6.   Select **Export to FEA** in the Output Grapher

7.   Select Mounting Lugs:3 > Click **OK**

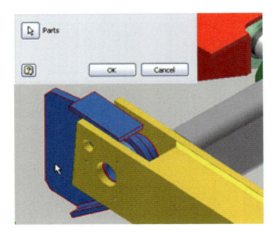

This component has now been added to the Stress Analysis environment.

There is no need to specify bearing load faces as they are already preselected. To see which face has been selected, right click the component 3894-4 Ramp Mounting Lugs:3 and select **Edit Load bearing Faces**.

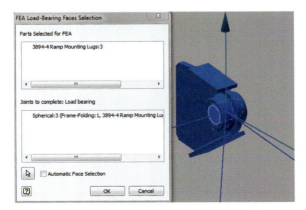

8. Close **Output Grapher** > Select **Construction Mode**

9. Select **Finish Dynamic Simulation** > Select **Environments** tab > Select **Stress Analysis**

10. Select **Create Simulation** > Select **Motion Loads Analysis**

11. Select the **Model State** tab > Select **Mount-Lug** for **Level of Detail** > Click **OK**

12. Click **OK** to **Grounded Part Warning**

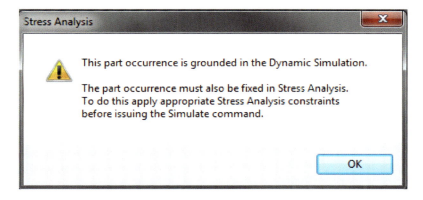

📝 This message states the part is grounded in dynamic simulation and therefore also needed to be restrained within the Stress Analysis Environment

Apply fixed constraints

13. Select **Fixed Constraint** from the **Constraints** panel

14. Select the 3 faces of Component **3894-4 Ramp Mounting Lugs:3** as shown to constrain the component > Click **OK**

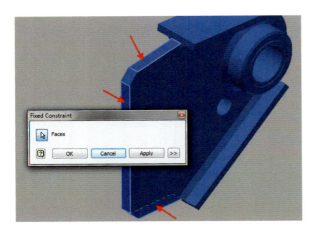

15. Select **Automatic Contacts** > Select **Mesh View**

 Select Automatic Contacts if running analysis for the first time even if it's a single part. It may help to speed up analysis

Run simulation and analyze

16. Select **Simulate** > Run **Analysis**

Analyze safety factor results

The following stress results appear.

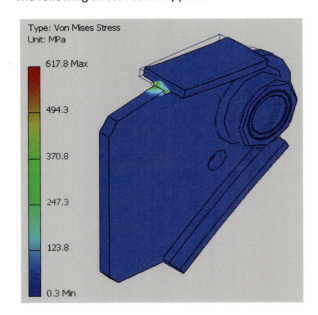

This stress display shows peak stresses around the top face, which was constrained. In reality, this lug is welded to a PFC channel at the fixed faces. Hence, the stresses that we will obtain will be

slightly higher, as these faces will have no movement, whereas in reality these faces will transfer some movement into the PFC channel. To remove the peak stress and to allow extra movement in the lug, we will apply frictional constraints at the top and bottom face, instead of fixed constraints.

Modify boundary conditions

17. Double click Fixed Constraints:1 > Deselect the top and bottom faces > Click **OK**

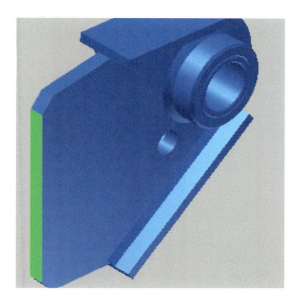

18. Select **Frictionless Constraint** > Select the top and bottom faces > Click **OK**

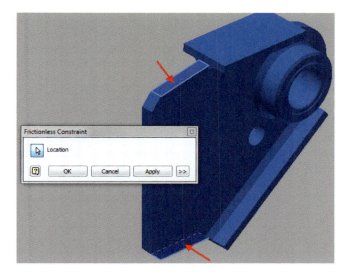

19. Select **Simulate** > Rerun **Analysis**

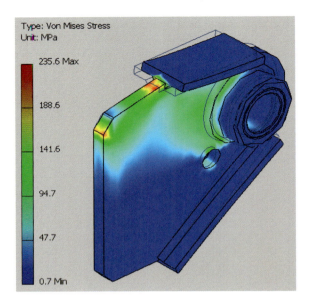

By applying Frictionless constraints we have removed the peak localized stress and introduced some extra movement in the lug. Therefore care should be taken when manipulating boundary conditions in addition to interpreting results.

20. Double Click **Safety Factor**

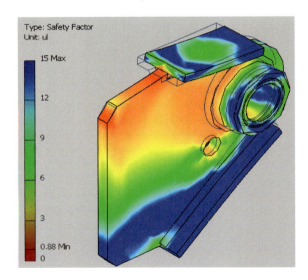

The minimum value of 0.9 suggests the component has failed. This does not represent reality, as the load is twice as big, as explained in the Dynamic Simulation course. So, we will alter the remote force by half. We do not need to alter the moment and body load as they are zero. Gravity does not need to be altered, either, as it is the same.

21. Right click Remote Force:1 > Select **Edit Remote Force Load**

22. Select **Use Vector Components**, and specify half the value of Fx and Fy vector components >
Click **OK**

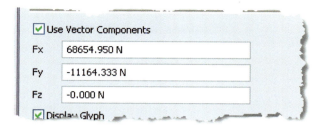

There is no need to edit remote point values

23. Select **Simulate** > Run **Analysis**

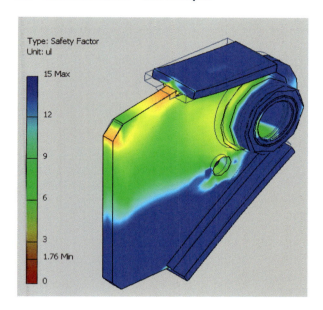

The safety factor has increased to 1.76. The safety factor is still lower than the limit and needs
to be increased. One option is to use a higher strength material.

CHAPTER 11
DP10 – Motion Load Transfer Analysis

Optimization

24. Select **Assign Materials** > Change the material to **Steel, High Strength Low Alloy** in the **Override Material** column > Click **OK**

Component	Original Material	Override Material	Safety Factor
▸ --¦ Ramp-Open (Mount-Lug)			
┆---¦ 3894-4 Ramp Mounting Lugs:3	Steel, Mild	Steel, High Strength Low Alloy	Yield Strength

(Assign Materials)

25. Select **Simulate** > Run **Analysis**

26. Select **Safety Factor**

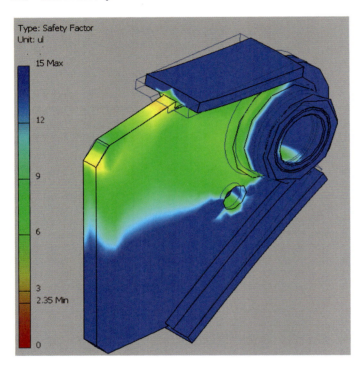

The safety factor has increased to approx 2.35, which means that the component is strong enough to withstand the full load.

27. Select **Finish Stress Analysis**

28. Close the file

DP11 – Multiple Motion Load Transfer

Structural Validation of Connecting Rod
(Design Problem Courtesy of 888 Racing Ltd)

Key features and workflows introduced in this design problem

	Key Features/Workflows
1	Motion loads – Multiple time steps
2	Modify joint position
3	Automatic convergence of results

Introduction

This design problem will look at the effective use of Dynamic Simulation to validate the structural integrity of the connecting rod. The force will be exported from the simulation study and will be directly used in the Stress Analysis environment, removing the need to apply loads and restraints.

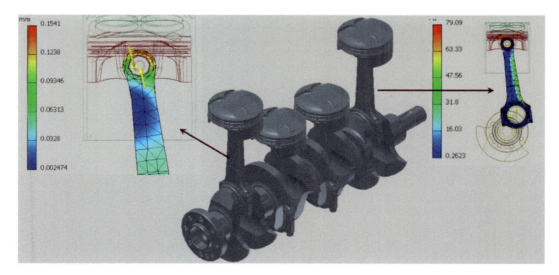

The main requirements of this design problem are to determine:

- Maximum stress in the connecting rod whilst in operation.
- Maximum deflection in the connecting rod.
- Factor of safety - for example, the fatigue life could be predicted.

SECTION 4 - Stress Analysis Design Problems using Motion Loads from Dynamic Simulation

CHAPTER 12

DP11 – Multiple Motion Load Transfer

In addition to the main requirements, the design criteria to be used for this design problem are the following:

- The material to be used is mild steel *
- The factor of safety required is 5
- Piston: minimum weight is 350g
- Conrod: minimum weight is 500g (including all bolts and bearings)
- Crank-shaft: minimum weight is 11.0kg

*Triple Eight Racing will actually use a higher strength grade of steel

Workflow of Design Problem 11

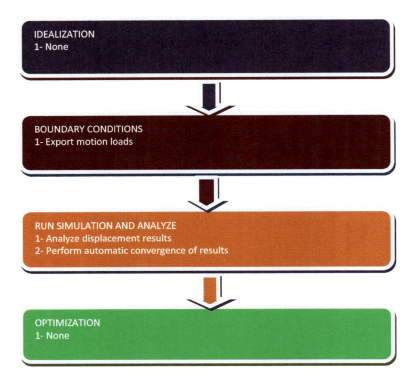

Idealization

The connecting rod has already been derived into a single part and hence no further simplification is required. In this design problem, the loads will be transferred from the Dynamic Simulation environment.

1. Open *completed*.iam

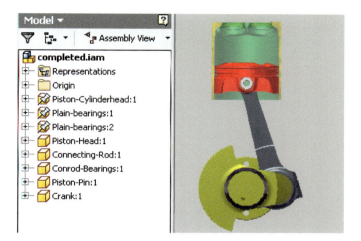

2. Select **Environments** tab > Select **Dynamic Simulation**

Boundary conditions

3. Play **Simulation** > Select **Output Grapher**

4. Right Click the Time data column > Select **Unselect all Curves**

5. Select Force for Revolutions:3 and Point-Line:4 joints

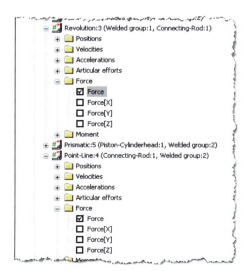

6. Right Click Force (Revolution:3) column > Select **Search Max**

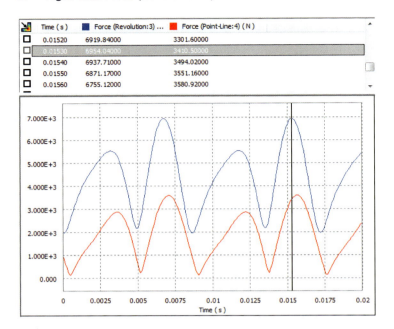

The maximum force for the Force (Revolution:3) joint is 6954 N and occurs at time 0.0153 seconds . We will export this force to the Stress Analysis environment. The value may differ.

Export motion loads

7. Tick in the **Export to FEA** column at 0.0153 seconds to export loads at this time frame

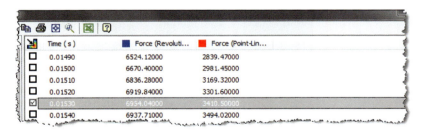

 This time step is now added

8. Right Click Force (Point-Line:4) column > Select **Search Max**

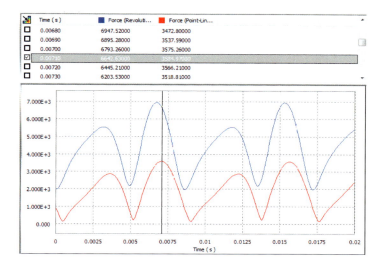

The maximum force for the Force (Point Line:4) joint is 3582 N and occurs at time 0.0071 seconds . As this force occurs at a different time, we will also export this force to the Stress Analysis environment.

9. Tick in the **Export to FEA** column at 0.00710 seconds to export loads at this time frame

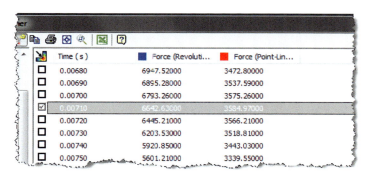

This time step is also added

10. Close **Output Grapher**

11. Select **Export to FEA**

12. Select Connecting Rod > Click **OK**

13. Select the face, as shown, to transfer the reaction loads of Joint 3 to this face

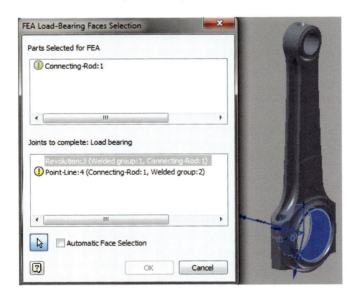

14. Select Joint 4 in the dialogue box > Select face on the other side of connecting rod

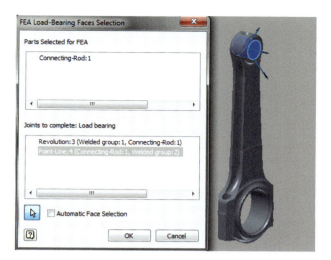

15. Click **OK** > Select **Finish Dynamic Simulation**

16. Select **Environments** tab > Select **Stress Analysis**

17. Select **Create Simulation** > Specify **Conrod-Analysis** for **Name** > Select **Motion Loads Analysis** > Click **OK**

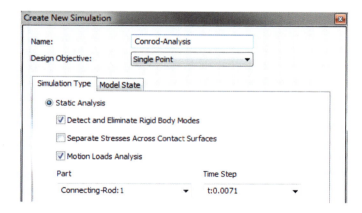

DP11 – Multiple Motion Load Transfer

The following loads will be created.

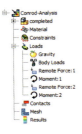
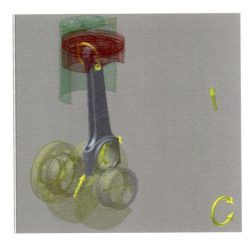

18. Select **Mesh View**

Run simulation and analyze

19. Select **Simulate** > Run **Analysis**

20. Select **Actual** for **Displacement Display**. The value may slightly differ

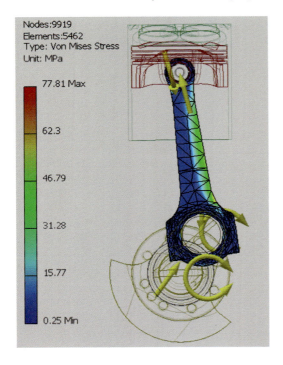

21. Double click **Displacement**. The value may slightly differ

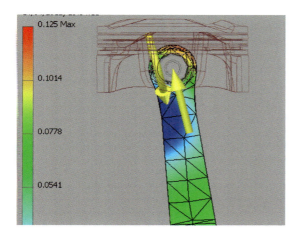

Analyze displacement results

Although we have performed a stress analysis, the motion loads transferred from the top of the connecting rod are not correct as they have induced a moment not acting directly through the centre of the conrod.

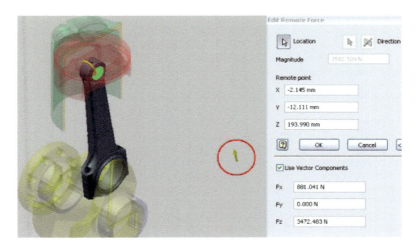

So, we need to alter this to see whether the results change.

22. Select **Finish Stress Analysis**

23. Select **Environments** tab > Select **Dynamic Simulation**

24. Select **Construction Mode** > Right Click **Point-Line:4** joint > Select **Edit**

25. For Component 1 Origin > Reselect point on conrod as shown > Click **OK**

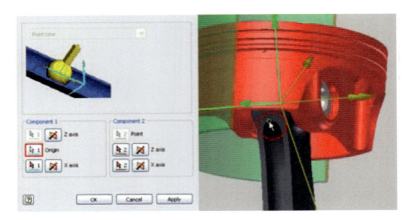

26. Play **Simulation** > Select **Construction Mode**

27. Select **Finish Dynamic Simulation**

28. Select **Environments** tab > Select **Stress Analysis**

29. Right Click **Loads** > Select **Update**

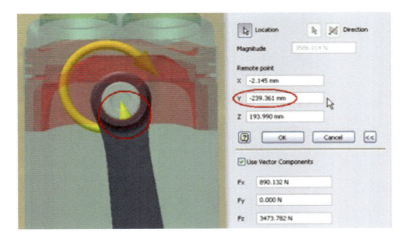

The force has now moved in-line with the connecting rod instead of being offset

30. Select **Simulate** > Run **Analysis**

31. Select **Actual for Displacement Scale**. The value may slightly differ

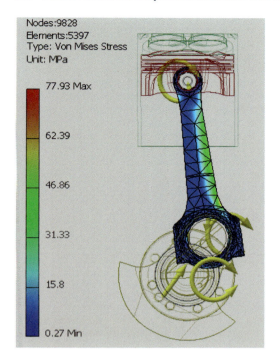

Even though the results did not change, you should be aware of the position of joints and their potential impact on the results.

Perform automatic convergence of results

Next, we need to determine whether the results have converged.

32. Select **Convergence Settings**

33. Specify 3 **Maximum number of h refinements** > Click **OK**

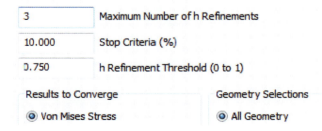

3	Maximum Number of h Refinements
10.000	Stop Criteria (%)
0.750	h Refinement Threshold (0 to 1)

Results to Converge	Geometry Selections
◉ Von Mises Stress	◉ All Geometry

DP11 – Multiple Motion Load Transfer

34. Select **Simulate** > Rerun **Simulation**

35. Select **Convergence Plot**

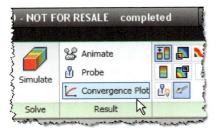

The graph below shows the maximum Von Mises Stress results have converged. The value may slightly differ

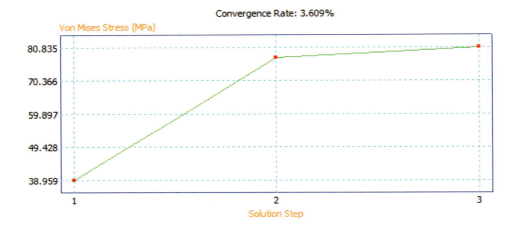

The convergence plot shows that the convergence has been achieved within the automatic P-refinement stage.

36. Close **Convergence Plot** > Double Click **Safety Factor**

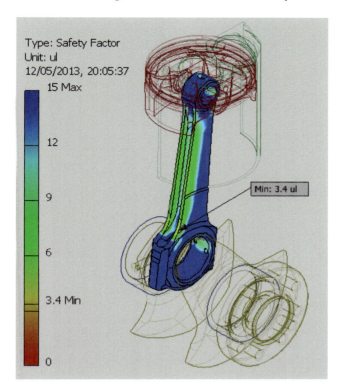

Now, repeat the above steps for the motion load transferred at time step 0.0153s and see whether the safety factor changes.

 Quicker to Copy simulation and change time step from 0.0710 to 0.0153s

37. Close File

Section 5 -
MODAL ANALYSIS
Design Problems
using SOLID ELEMENTS

DP12 – Modal Analysis

Modal Analysis of TV Camera Arm attached to Helicopter
(Design Problem courtesy of Aerospace Design Facilities Ltd)

Key features and workflows introduced in this design problem

	Key Features/Workflows
1	Modal shapes and natural frequencies
2	Modal optimization

Introduction

Aerospace Design Facilities Ltd, based in the UK, is a European Aviation Safety Agency (EASA) FIC approved design organization for both helicopters and fixed wing aircraft. Aerospace Design Facilities Ltd also supplies bespoke design and manufacturing services to the film industry. One typical example of their work is designing camera mounts to be placed on helicopters, as shown below.

A major consideration during the design of a camera mount on helicopters is the need to ensure that the vibrations produced by the dynamics of the airframe (rotating components) are not amplified. Generally, the camera systems have been designed to be either hard mounted (i.e. they can cope with the amplitude and frequencies) or attached via an isolation mount. The basic design of the structure to support the camera must be evaluated for its natural frequency response with the camera system installed, and without if the structure is to be flown without a camera system attached.

CHAPTER 13
DP12 – Modal Analysis

The camera arm design is attached to a helicopter having a three-bladed main rotor with a nominal speed of 393rpm. Therefore, the dominant frequencies will be

393 rpm / 60s = 6.55 Hz

And as there are 3 rotor blades, there will be 3 passes of the blade in one revolution producing a further dominant frequency of

6.55 Hz x3 = 19.65 Hz

The design of the camera mounts needs to cope with the structural aspects of aerodynamic crash loads; however, the first part of the analysis should be an evaluation of natural frequencies.

Although there are many other considerations involved with this design, this chapter will only investigate two of the natural frequencies that need to be avoided during the design of this camera mount:

Frequency 1 (R1) = **6.55**Hz
Frequency 2 (R3) = **19.65**Hz

The major design restrictions for the camera mount are as follows;

1. The position of the fixing points for the camera mount and the camera are fixed.
2. The maximum weight of the design, including camera, should not exceed 50Kg.
3. The camera offset position relative to the neutral axis of the camera arm is restricted by clearance to both ground and helicopter. In an ideal situation, the position of the centre of gravity of the camera needs to be in line with the neutral axis of the mount arm to minimize vibration.

Workflow of Design Problem 12

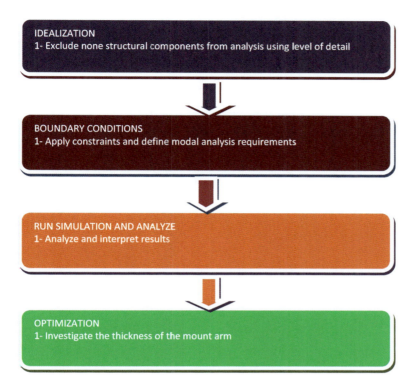

Idealization

The main weight of camera mount assembly comprises the camera (30.5kg) and mount design. The mass of the fasteners is small and to simplify the analysis further all fasteners and associated components are excluded from the simulation. Furthermore, the model of the camera and connecting plate has been simplified by suppressing radii, holes, etc. All this idealization of the camera mount is saved as a level of detail, avoiding the need to suppress non-key components and features in the Stress Analysis environment. Two levels of detail have been created: one without the camera and the second with the camera. This will allow us to analyze and compare the modal shape, including natural frequencies, of both models. Initially we will have a look at the natural frequencies of the arm.

CHAPTER 13
DP12 – Modal Analysis

1.   Open *Mount Assembly*.iam

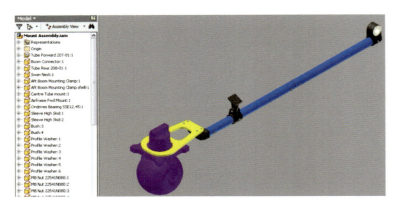

Boundary conditions

2.   Select **Environments** tab > Select **Stress Analysis**

3.   Select **Create Simulation** > Specify **Arm** for **Name** > Type 4 for Number of Modes > Select **Enhanced Accuracy**

4.   Select **Model State** tab > Select **Arm** for **Level of Detail** > Click **OK**

5.   Select **Fixed Constraints** > Select the face as shown > Click **OK**

6. Select **Pin Constraints** > Select the faces as shown > Click **OK**

7. Select **Automatic Contacts** to create contacts between components

Five contacts will be created in total.

Some contacts will need to be created manually between components that have larger clearances due to excluding components from simulation (including washers/connectors etc.)

8. Select **Manual Contact** > Select faces as shown > Click **Apply**

9. Repeat Step 9 for faces on other side of the clamp > Click **Apply**

10. Select the two faces to connect the tubes together > Click **OK**

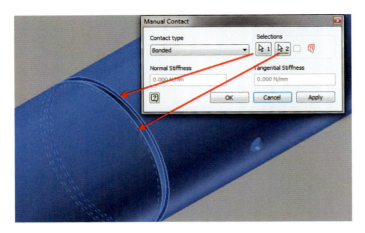

The following three manual contacts will be created

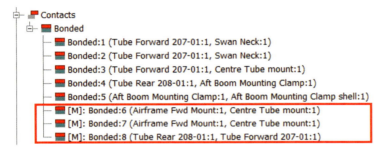

11. Select **Mesh Settings** > Specify 0.02 for **Average Element Size** > Check **Create Curved Mesh Elements** > Uncheck **Use part based measure for Assembly mesh** > Click **OK**

12. Select **Mesh View**

A total of 73,375 nodes and 38,280 elements will be created. There may be slight variation.

Use a relatively small mesh size to produce a more accurate modal analysis.

Run Simulation and Analyze

13. Select **Simulate** > Run **Analysis** > Unselect **Mesh View**

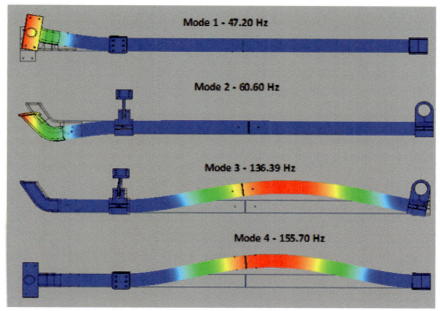

These are the first four modes, defined by the modal shape and natural frequencies, of the arm without the camera. It is important to note that all calculated frequencies are much higher than the R1 and R3 frequencies, which means that the arm without the camera will produce minimal vibration under normal helicopter operating conditions.

Now we will see the effect of adding the camera to the arm and see the first four modes again.

14. Right click **Arm** > Select **Copy Simulation**

15. Right click **Arm:1** > Select **Edit Simulation Properties** > Specify **Arm-with-Camera** for **Name** > Select **Model State** >Select **Arm-with-Camera** for **Level of Detail** > Click **OK**

16. Right click **Contacts** >Select **Update Automatic Contacts**

Two more contacts will be created between the camera assembly and arm; ten in total.

17. Select **Mesh View**

18. Select **Simulate** > Run **Analysis** > Unselect **Mesh View**

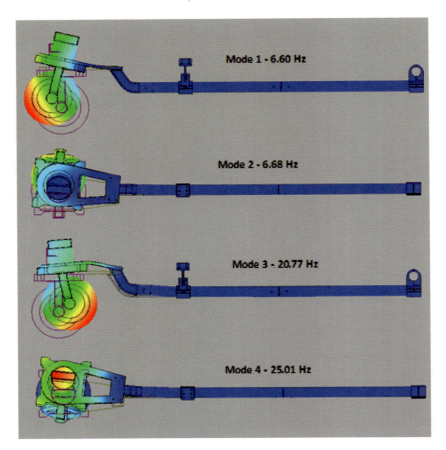

We can now clearly see that the fundamental frequency (Mode 1) has significantly reduced from 47.20 Hz to 6.60 Hz, and this applies to all other three other modes as well. Also, it is important to note that Mode 1,2 and 3 frequencies are very close to rotor speeds. This means that we need to increase the frequencies.

This can be achieved in a number of ways including specifying different material properties, increasing the tube thicknesses, moving the mount positions, and altering geometry of swan neck part to move the position of the centre of the gravity of camera in line with the neutral axis of the tubes. Some of these options are limited by the camera ground clearance, interference with the helicopter airframe, and the overall weight of the assembly.

Here, we will pursue the option of increasing the thickness of the arm to alter the natural frequencies.

 Young's modulus, density and Poison's ratio are the only material properties taken into account when performing a modal analysis.

Optimization

To change tube thicknesses we can either go back into each component or change the sketches, or alternatively we can use parametric optimization within stress analysis to see the effect of tube thicknesses. The latter option is more efficient and, depending on results, can allow the ability to replace and update existing model parameter values with the new stress analysis parameters.

 Create user parameters when using parametric option.

19. Right click **Arm-with-Camera:**1 > Select **Edit Simulation Properties**

20. Change **Design Objective** to **Parametric Dimension**

21. Select **Simulate** > Run **Analysis,** this will update results

22. Right click the **Tube Forward 2071-01:1** Part > Select **Show Parameters** > Check **Tube_thickness** user parameter > Click **OK**

23. Right Click the **Tube Forward 208-01:1** Part > Select **Show Parameters** > Check **Tube_ thickness** user parameter > Click **OK**

24. Right click **Swan Neck:1** Part > Select **Show Parameters** > Check **Tube_thickness** user parameter > Click **OK**

25. Select **Parametric Table** > Add **Mass Design Constraint**

This will help us keep a control on the mass limit of 50Kg.

26. Specify the following values for Tube_ thicknesses

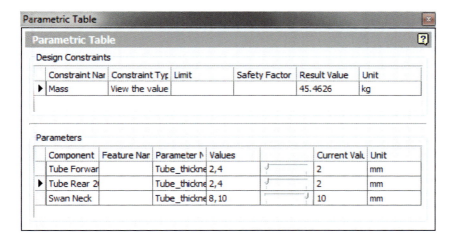

We are going to increase the main tubes of the camera mount assembly from 2 to 4. The Swan neck component is attached to inside of the tubes and, to avoid interference, will need to reduce its thickness by the same amount of (2mm).

CHAPTER 13

DP12 – Modal Analysis

27. Set the **Current Values** for each parameter as shown

Parameters

Component Name	Feature Name	Parameter Name	Values		Current Value	Unit
Tube Forward 207-0		Tube_thickness	2,4		4	mm
Tube Rear 208-01		Tube_thickness	2,4		4	mm
▶ Swan Neck		Tube_thickness	8,10		8	mm

28. Right Click in any of the rows > Select **Generate Current Configuration** > Select **Simulate this configuration** > Select **Run**

 This will analyze model based on current values set by the user, with the aid of the slider

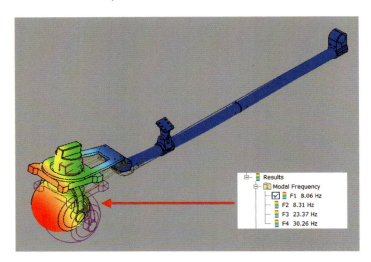

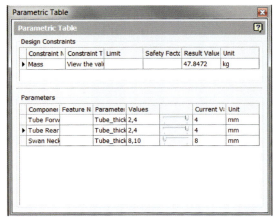

We can clearly see that the frequencies have increased by doubling the wall thickness of the tube and the mass of 47.8472kg, from within the parametric table, is below the 50 kg limit. The frequencies can be further enhanced by making the tube even more thicker or even change to a stronger material

29. Close File

Section 6 -

FRAME ANALYSIS
Essentials
& Design Problems
using BEAM ELEMENTS

The Frame Analysis Environment

Frame Analysis Overview

Frame Analysis is normally associated with analyzing large structures mainly comprising uniform cross-section channels/frames. Typical examples include bridges, structural platforms, towers etc. Some examples are illustrated below.

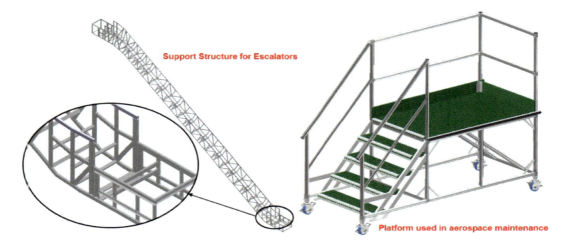

Support Structure for Escalators

Platform used in aerospace maintenance

Frame Analysis, within Autodesk Inventor Simulation, allows us to define criteria for static and modal analysis, including prestressing. In addition, **Frame Analysis** uses beam elements instead of the 3D tetrahedron and thin elements used within the Stress Analysis environment.

A simple beam element comprises of two nodes, one at each end, and has three translational and three rotational degrees of freedom (DOF); six in total.

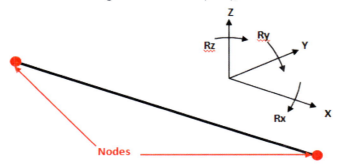

Some reasons for using beam elements rather than tetrahedron elements are reduced model sizes, reduced number of elements used, and faster analysis times. This can be demonstrated by the following example in which a beam is fixed at one end and a 1000N load applied at the other end.

CHAPTER 14
The Frame Analysis Environment

The results of both stress and **Frame Analysis** are summarized below (the results are dependent on factors such as computer speed).

	Displacement (mm)	Stress (max) (MPa_	Mesh-time* (s)	N° of elements	Analysis-time (s)
Stress Analysis	1.970	53.32	8	5780	6
Frame Analysis	1.949	51.46	1	10	1
Theoretical Results	1.949	51.46	-	-	-

*A default mesh of 0.1 **Average Element Size** was used within the Stress Analysis environment.

These results illustrate that a simple structure, such as an I-beam, can have a significant impact on the model sizes and analysis times. For this simple reason it is normal practice to analyze a thin structure, with uniform cross-section, with beam elements. Another advantage of using beam elements is that there is no stress singularities/stress concentrations to overcome. These stress concentrations probably cause the slight difference in the stress results when compared with the theoretical result (less than 5%).

Frame Analysis Workflow

The process of creating an analysis (both stress and modal) involves four core steps:

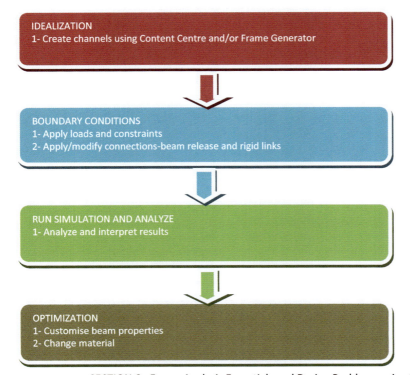

SECTION 6 - Frame Analysis Essentials and Design Problems using Beam Elements

Frame Analysis User Interface

Frame Analysis can only be accessed from the Assembly environment via either the **Environments** or **Design** tab.

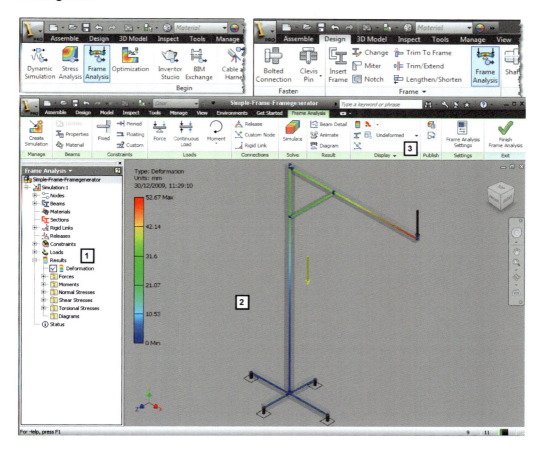

1. **Frame Analysis** Browser
2. **Frame Analysis** Graphic Window
3. **Frame Analysis** Panel

Frame Analysis Browser

Displays the simulations with the part or assembly and simulation parameters in a hierarchical view with nested levels of features and attributes information. You can:

- Copy whole simulations or simulation objects between simulations.
- Right-click on a node for context menu options.
- Expand the folders, select the nodes, and see the selection cross-highlight in the graphic region.

Frame Analysis Graphic Window

Displays the model geometry and simulation results. Updates to show current status of the simulation, including applying boundary conditions and loads with the help of view manipulation tools

CHAPTER 14
The Frame Analysis Environment

Frame Analysis Panel

Dynamic Simulation Tab	Workflow Stage	Description
Create Simulation — Manage	Step 1	**Create Simulation** – Here you decide whether you need to create a stress, modal or a parametric analysis.
Update, Properties, Material — Beams	Step 2	**Beams** – Create and apply materials for the components if not already defined in the Part environment
Fixed, Pinned, Floating, Custom — Constraints		**Constraints** – Represent how a part is fixed or attached to other parts in reality, and thus how their motion is restricted
Force, Continuous Load, Moment — Loads		**Loads** - Represent the external forces that are exerted on a component. During normal use, the component is expected to withstand these loads and continue to perform as intended
Release, Custom Node, Rigid Link — Connections		**Connections** – Create contacts between components automatically or manually. There are seven types of contacts, including bonded
Simulate — Solve	Step 3	**Solve** – Run the simulation to analyze results as a consequence of defining materials, constraints and loads
Beam Detail, Animate, Diagram, Probe — Result		**Results** – View the stress and deformation results to provide an informed decision regarding whether the component will function under the defined loads and constraints.
Color Bar, Smooth Shading, Beam Labels, Adjusted x1, Node Labels, Probe Labels — Display ▾	-	**Display** – Modify color plots including displaying maximum and minimum values
Report, Export — Publish	-	**Publish** – Generate an html report of the results to share
Frame Analysis Settings — Settings	-	**Settings** – Predefine initial settings including contact tolerance and mesh settings

Manage tab

This is the first step in creating a frame analysis study.

Create Simulation

Here you can define whether you want to carry out single static analysis, a modal analysis, or a parametric study –including the option of selecting different levels of detail.

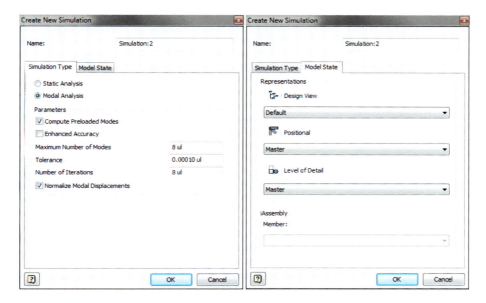

Simulation Type – Here you define whether a stress or modal analysis is to be carried out.

Model State – For an assembly you can choose any design view and level of detail on which to perform the analysis.

Parameters (modal analysis only) – When performing modal analysis, there are three settings that can be defined

Compute Preloaded Modes –This is checked by default and calculates the modes of the model when in the loaded condition. Modes under the preloaded condition tend to have higher natural frequencies than models that are not preloaded.

Maximum Number of Modes – This calculates the number of modes, including modal shape and natural frequencies, required; the default is set to 8.

Tolerance – Here you can define the accuracy of the results required. The iterative solver goes through repetitive analysis until the difference in the results is within this tolerance setting.

Number of Iterations – Here you define the number of repetitive analysis required. The default value is set to 10.

Beams tab

Update

This becomes active when the model has been changed, for example in the assembly environment, and thus requires an update.

Properties

Normally most components will have their materials assigned within the Part environment, thus removing the need to assign material, as they will come across directly from the Part environment.

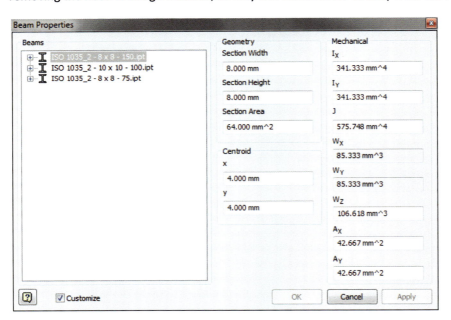

Basic Properties – The width and height are the overall dimensions of the cross-section of the beam; for example, a diameter of 10mm will have a width and height of 10mm. The area is the true cross-section area of the beam.

Centroid – The position of the centroid with reference to the beam coordinate system.

Mechanical – These values provide details of the second moment of area (I_x, I_y), polar second moment of area (I_z),section modulus (W_x, W_y, W_z) and Shear Stress (A_x, A_y)

Below are two examples of simple shapes with their associated cross-sectional mechanical properties.

	2nd Moment of Area	Section Modulus
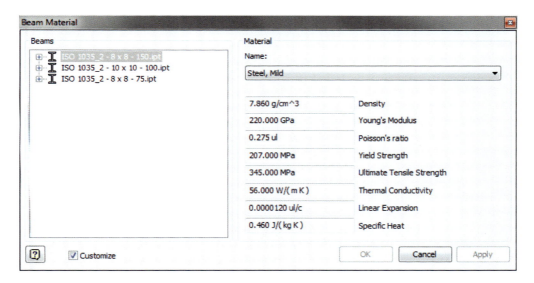	$\dfrac{\pi D^4}{64}$	$\dfrac{\pi D^3}{32}$
	$\dfrac{b d^3}{12}$	$\dfrac{b d^2}{6}$

Material

The materials of the beams are normally pre-assigned when you create frames using Frame Generator and Content Centre. These are the material properties that are read by the Frame Analysis environment

If the material is inadequately defined then the simulation will not run and an error message will be displayed in the Status folder in the browser. The material can be changed within Frame Analysis using the **Customize** button.

 The customize will not let you alter the alter the material properties including density, young's modulus etc

Constraints tab

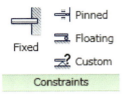

Constraints can be created by either using the heads up display (HUD) or constraints dialogue box, as illustrated below.

 When a beam is selected, to place any constraint, an internal node is created that connects the constraint to the beam.

Fixed constraint

Fixed constraint removes all translation and rotational degrees of freedom of the selected node or beam. Both nodes and beams can be selected to specify the origin. The **Offset** parameter will only be activated if a beam is selected to define **Origin**. The **Offset** can be specified either in absolute or relative values. A value of 0.5, when **Relative** is selected, will place the constraint in the middle of the beam. Fixed constraints simulate bolted and welded connections, and joint as illustrated below

Bolted Connection   **Welded Connection**

Pinned constraint

Pinned Constraint only removes all translational degrees of freedom of the selected node or beam. Both nodes and beams can be selected to specify the **Origin**. The **Offset** parameter will only be activated if a beam is selected to define **Origin**. The offset can either be specified in either absolute or relative values. An absolute value of 100 mm will place the constraint in the middle of a 200 mm beam. Pin constraints simulate hinge and pin-hole connections, and joints as illustrated below:

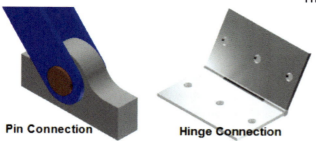

Pin Connection   **Hinge Connection**

 A single pin-type constraint will behave more like a spherical joint/constraint, as it has three degrees of rotation. However, in most applications there will be more than one constraint and in such circumstances the constraint will behave more like a pin constraint, as its rotational degrees of freedom will be restricted.

Floating pinned constraint

Floating Pinned Constraint restricts rotation and translation in one plane only for a selected node or beam. Both nodes and beams can be selected to specify the **Origin**. Additionally, the direction can be specified by selecting work axes, work planes or beam. The **Offset** parameter will only be activated if a beam is selected to define the **Origin**. The **Offset** can either be specified in absolute or relative values. An absolute value of 100 mm will place the constraint at one-third of the length along a 300 mm beam. The angle of the plane – where the constraint has one degree of displacement – can also be specified in addition to the angle of the constraint – with reference to the default Z axis. Floating pinned constraints simulate rollers, wheels and smooth surface-type joints, as illustrated below.

The table below is a summary of the supports and connections the degrees of freedom of which is fixed depending on the type of standard support/constraint used.

		Translational d.o.f			Rotational d.o.f		
		X	Y	Z	Rx	Ry	Rz
1	Fixed support	√	√	√	√	√	√
2	Pinned connection	√	√	√			
3	Floating support *		√		√		√

Finally, below is a summary of the types of results available, including reactions and moments, depending on the type of standard constraint used.

		Reacting Forces			Reacting Moments		
		Rx	Ry	Rz	Mx	My	Mz
1	Fixed support	√	√	√	√	√	√
2	Pinned connection	√	√	√			
3	Floating support *		√				

* Fixed and loaded in a plane normal to the Y-axis

Custom constraint

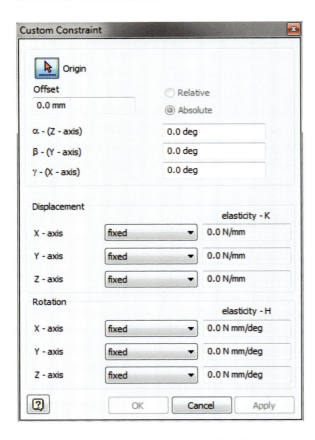

Custom constraint is the only constraint that allows control of its six degrees of freedom: For example, a custom constraint could be used to define a pin constraint by fixing its two degrees of rotation and three degrees of translation. **Custom constraint** also allows the specification of stiffness (elasticity), enabling simulation of connections between moving components.

Below are the details of all the options:

α - (Z-axis) – Specify the angle of constraint rotation about the Z axis.
β - (Y-axis) – Specify the angle of constraint rotation about the Y axis.
γ - (X-Axis) – Specify the angle of constraint rotation about the X axis.

Fixed - Means that the joint behaves like a fixed constraint
Uplift none - Means that the degree of freedom (rotation and displacement) is free and not restricted.
Uplift+ - Means that the degree of freedom (rotation and displacement) is free only in the positive direction with respect to the beam coordinate system (local).
Uplift- - Means that the degree of freedom (rotation and displacement) is free only in the negative direction with respect to the beam coordinate system (local).

Refer to the image below to see the consequences of changing uplift settings.

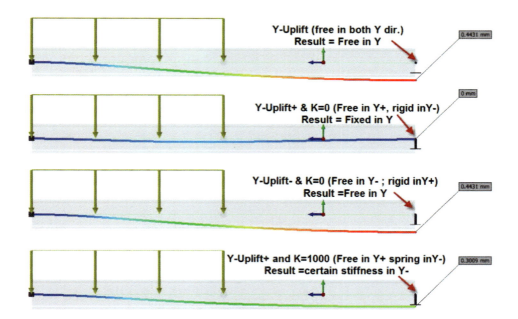

Loads tab

Force

To fully define a force, an origin, magnitude, and direction are required. **Direction** can be specified by selecting either the beam or axis. Alternatively, the direction can be specified by specifying **Angle of Plane** and **Angle in Plane**, where **Angle of Plane** rotates the XY plane of where the load is defined and **Angle in Plane** defines the angle of force from the Z axes. The **Offset** is only available if the beam is both selected and can be defined in absolute and relative values; for example, a relative value of 0.5 will place the force in the middle of the beam.

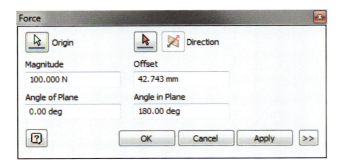

Below is an example of force being defined using **Vector** values.

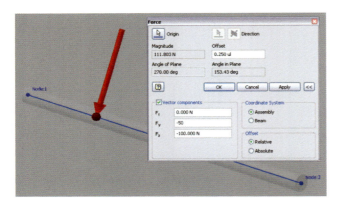

Continuous load

To fully define a continuous load, an origin, magnitude and direction are required. **Direction** can be specified by selecting either the beam or axis. Alternatively, the direction can also be specified by specifying **Angle of Plane** and **Angle in Plane**, where **Angle of Plane** rotates the XY plane of where the load is defined and **Angle in Plane** defines the angle of force from the Z axes.

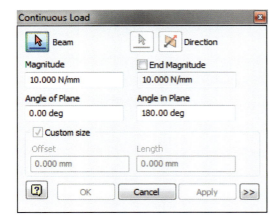

A variable load can be defined by enabling End Magnitude, and specifying two different Magnitude values.

Below is an example of a continuous load being defined using the heads up display (HUD)

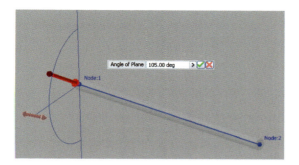

Moment

Moment (general)

To fully define a general moment, an origin, magnitude, and direction are required. **Direction** can be specified by selecting either the beam or axis, including specifying moment in the beam and assembly coordinate system. Alternatively, the direction can be specified by specifying **Angle of Plane** and **Angle in Plane**, where **Angle of Plane** rotates the XY plane of where the moment is acting and **Angle in Plane** defines the angle of moment from the Z axes. The offset is only available if the beam is selected and can be defined in absolute and relative values; for example, a relative value of 0.5 will place the force in the middle of the beam.

Bending and axial moment can also be defined by using general moment. Below is an example of a bending moment being created using HUD.

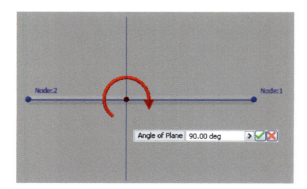

Bending Moment

Creates a bending moment on the selected beam and is applied in the plane parallel to the beam axis. It works in the beam coordinate system only and requires fewer input values than the general **Moment** dialogue box

Axial Moment

Create an axial moment on the specified beam and is applied in the plane perpendicular to the beam axis. It works in beam coordinate system only and, again, requires fewer input values than the general **Moment** dialogue box.

Example 1 – Cantilever model results compared with hand calculations

The following example is of a cantilever loaded at one end and fixed at the other.

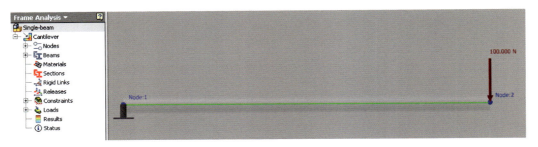

The beam, made out of mild steel (E = 220GPa), is 200mm long and 10mm diameter. With a 100N load applied, the maximum deflection and bending Stress are 2.469mm and 203.7MPa, respectively.

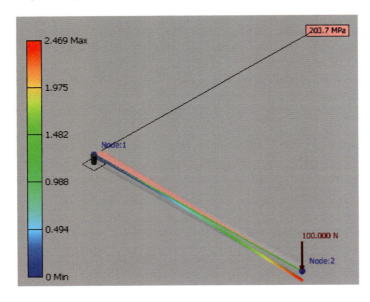

As a comparison, the maximum deflection and bending stress based on theoretical results, using the following formulae, are **2.469**mm **and 203.7**MPa, respectively.

Maximum Deflection $= WL^3/3EI$

Where;

W is load
L is length
E is Young's modulus
I is second moment of area

I for a circle is

$\pi D^4/64 = \pi * 0.01^4/64 = 4.908 \times 10^{-10}$

Based on the classical bending stress formula

$$\frac{M}{I} = \frac{\sigma}{y}$$

Maximum Deflection $= \dfrac{100 \times 0.2^3}{3 \times 220 \times 10^9 \times 4.908 \times 10^{-10}} = 0.002469$

Where:

M is Max bending moment = F x L =100x0.2 = 20Nm
σ is Max Stress
y is distance of neutral axis

Maximum σ = 20 x 0.005/4.908 x 10^{-10} = 203.7 x 10^6 N/m^2

TRY IT! – Open *Singlebeam.iam*

Example 2 – Simply supported beam created with custom constraint

The model used here is the as in Example 1, except that it is simply supported by pinned constraints at either end, with a load applied in the middle.

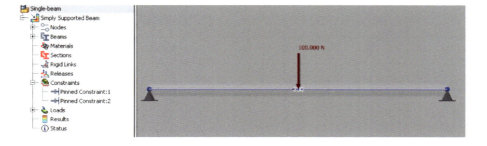

CHAPTER 14

The Frame Analysis Environment

With a 100N load applied, the maximum deflection and bending Stress are 0.1543mm and 50.93MPa, respectively.

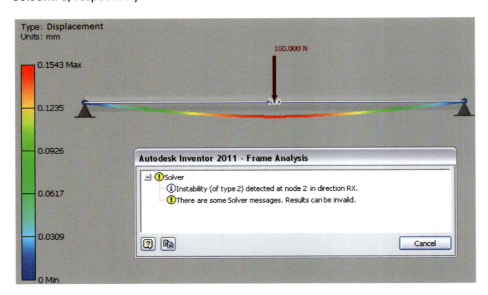

Although the results are correct based on the theoretical results, a warning appears detailing that the beam is free to rotate about its axis. This is due to the fact that applying a second pinned constraint on the other end of the beam has restricted the Y and Z (global) rotational degrees of freedom of both constraints. However, none of the constraints restrict motion about the axis of the beam.

To avoid the warning, we can replace one of the pinned constraints with a custom constraint, with all displacements and rotation about the axis of the beam fixed.

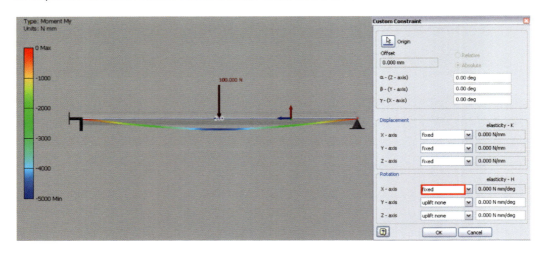

TRY IT! – Open *Singlebeam.iam*

Connections tab

Release
Custom Node
Rigid Link
Connections

Release

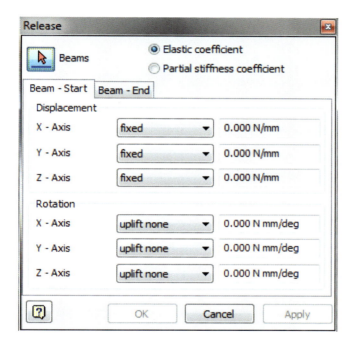

Beam release allows the release of rotational and translational degree of freedom in beam connections that have been created automatically; by default, beam end connections are rigid. For example, by releasing the rotational degrees of freedom; the fixed connection will convert to a pinned connection at the beam ends, thus removing moments in the beam. Refer to the beam release example. In addition to releasing degrees of freedom, elastic coefficients can also be specified to create stiffness at the beam ends, enabling some flexibility at the connections. When **Partial stiffness coefficient** is selected, value of 1.0 will mean no release and a value of 0 will mean maximum release.

When there are two or more adjoining beams, one of them should be fixed without a release at that beam end, as constraint already contains information about boundary conditions of adjoining beam.

While editing, the beam coordinate systems is displayed near the start end of the beam.

Fixed - Means that the joint behaves like a fixed constraint.

CHAPTER 14
The Frame Analysis Environment

Uplift none - Means that the degree of freedom (rotation and displacement) is free and not restricted.

Uplift+ - Means that the degree of freedom (rotation and displacement) is free only in the positive direction with respect to beam coordinate system (local).

Uplift- - means that the degree of freedom (rotation and displacement) is free only in the negative direction with respect to beam coordinate system (local).

Example 3 – Releasing moments in Structure using Beam Release

In this example, the following frame is loaded as shown.

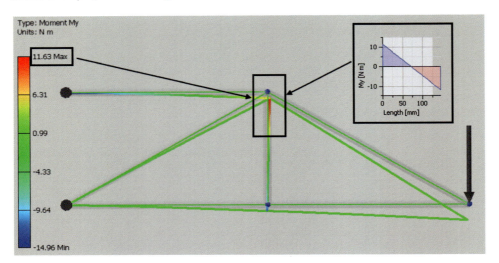

The maximum bending in the vertical member is 11.63Nm and, again, this is due to the frame member not having any rotational degree of freedom. In this example there are no rigid links, as in the previous example, were the rotational degree of freedom were released. This is due to the fact this truss frame has members with no end treatments; hence no gaps resulted between the members. Nevertheless, we can achieve the same effect by using the beam release command.

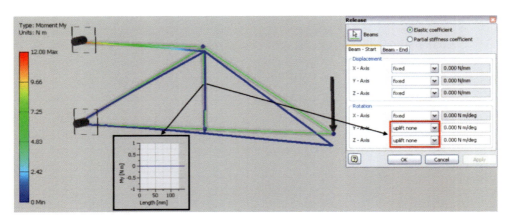

As we can see, by releasing rotation in the y and z axes for both ends of the beam has resulted in zero moment in the beam.

Releasing rotational degrees of freedom of the rigid link about y axis would have also sufficed to remove moments.

TRY IT! – Open *Truss.iam*

Custom Node

Custom nodes can be created anywhere along a beam and can be used to place forces and create rigid links. They are not graphically different from automatically converted nodes in the browser. However, we can assign different color in the **Frame Analysis Settings**.

Rigid link

Rigid links are used to join disconnected beams together. A rigid link comprises of a parent node and a child node. All displacement and rotations of the parent node are passed on to the child node; for example, compatibility between both nodes is maintained by the parent node. Displacements and rotations defined for a rigid link can be changed; for example, the **Rigid Link** setting below will maintain translation only between the nodes.

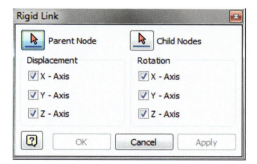

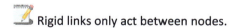 Rigid links only act between nodes.

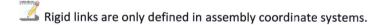 Rigid links are only defined in assembly coordinate systems.

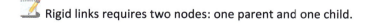 Rigid links requires two nodes: one parent and one child.

The Frame Analysis Environment

Below is an example of how two simple beams are connected together using rigid links.

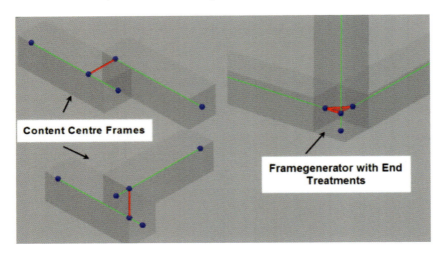

 Use Frame Generator to create frames if the frames are to have end treatments, as this will have an impact on the creation of rigid links between mitered/butt connected beams.

Below is an example of how four beams with end treatments, using Frame Generator, are connected with rigid links.

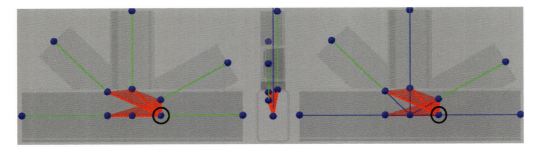

 A parent node is one in which all rigid links have a common connection point.

The blue lines are the axes used to create offset frames using Frame Generator and the green lines are the beam elements created in Frame Analysis based on the true neutral axis of the beam. Therefore, it is important to note that the beams elements are not necessarily created on the same axis on which the frames were originally created, with the exception of, for example, circular and square members. The above image shows a typical frame structure connection used in the Kone Escalator Support Structure as seen in the last chapter.

 Further information on how rigid links are connected between beams is available from the Autodesk Inventor Simulation **Help** file

Example 4 – Simple frame in which beams connected without using rigid links

The following support frame example is loaded at one end and fixed at the other end. Further, the example is created using Frame Generator with no end treatments. The deformation results show a maximum deflection of 2.035mm and a maximum normal stress of 118.8MPa.

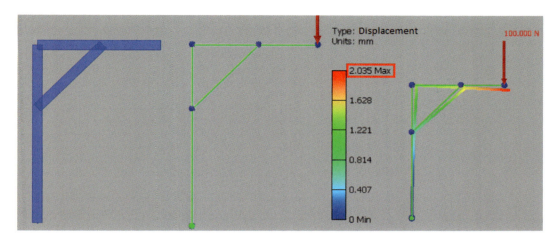

> # TRY IT! – Open *Simple-Frame.iam*

Example 5 – Frame Generator in which beams connected using rigid links

Now the same example with frame generator end treatments is simulated again.

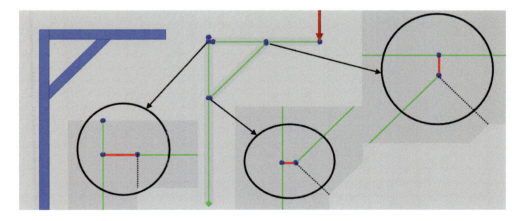

The immediate difference, even before we run the analysis, is the creation of the red rigid links. These links are automatically created and join the disconnected beams, due to trimming. The beams are extracted based on the neutral axis position and their length are defined by the intersection of longest face on the solid beam with a plane perpendicular to the neutral axis (see above). As a result of this, the rigid links are created between the beam elements using the shortest

CHAPTER 14
The Frame Analysis Environment

possible distance. However, the difference in the results is negligible as the maximum deformation and stress is 2.039mm and 118.8MPa, respectively.

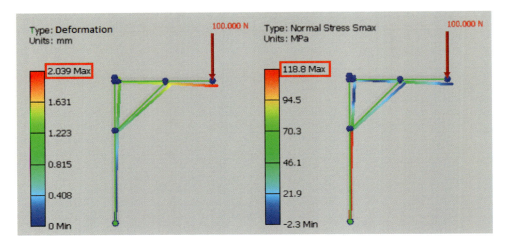

The reason for this similar result is that cross-section of the beams is very small compared to the length of the beam. In most structural applications this will always be the case, hence the reason for using beam elements rather than solid elements.

If the example is further analyzed, the beam connecting the horizontal and vertical beam is shown to have moments as shown below.

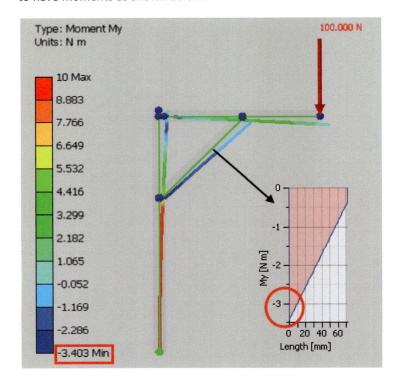

The reason for these moments is that the beam completely fixed and thus does not allow for beam rotations at the end, as would a pinned connection. To isolate moments in the beam, the rotational degrees of freedom of the rigid links connecting the beams can be released.

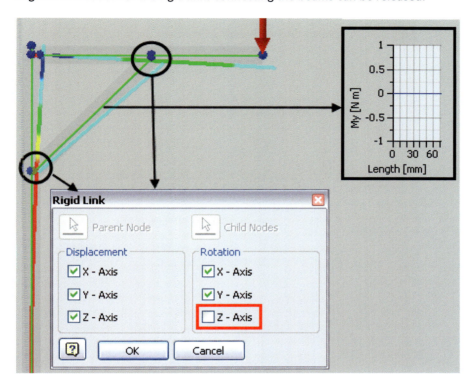

Rotation about the Z-axis (global coordinate system) is released and as thus removes moments completely in the beam. The stress (axial) now induced in the beam is completely due axial loading and not bending.

TRY IT! – Open *Simple-Framegenerator.iam*

Result tab

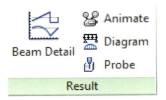

Beam detail

Beam Detail allows quick analysis of the details of the results for selected beams including maximum bending and forces.

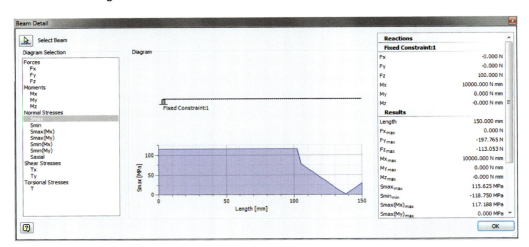

Animate

Creates a video file of the animation.

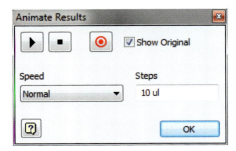

If **Show Original** is selected then the original model shape is visible during animation playback. On the other hand, if the option is not selected, the original wireframe is presented as an overlay on the deformed model. This option is checked by default.

 For a smoother display, increase the number of steps. You can specify any value between 1 and 100.

Diagram

Plots specific results, as diagrams, on beam models, result types include maximum forces and moments.

Multiple diagrams can be applied at the same time for the selected beam. The diagrams are plotted according to the beam local coordinate system and on the undeformed beams. The graphs that would normally be displayed along the beam axis are displayed along Y or Z axis of the beam coordinate system (in plane XY or XZ).

The complete list of result display available are shown below

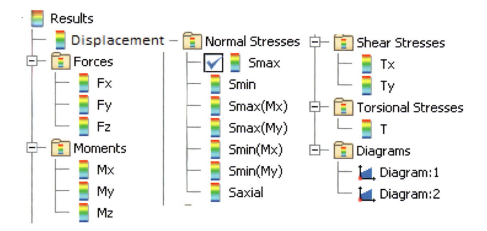

CHAPTER 14
The Frame Analysis Environment
The following show a diagram of the structural beam model

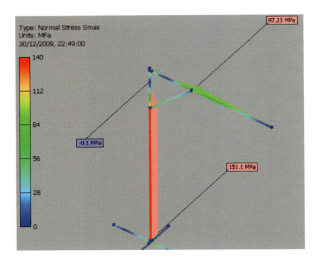

Probe
Allows users to create probe labels at user specified locals

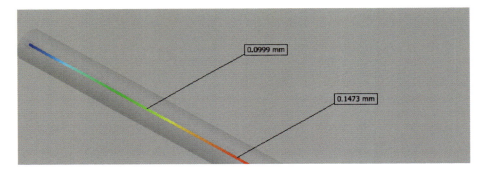

Display tab

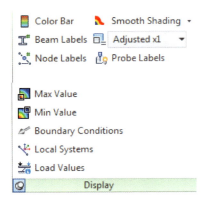

Color bar
The **Color Bar** is probably the most important tool within the **Display** panel and, when effectively used, can help with understanding the results with ease. It can be displayed in various locations in

the graphic window using the **Position** setting. The maximum and minimum threshold values can be altered by unchecking the **Maximum** and **Minimum** values.

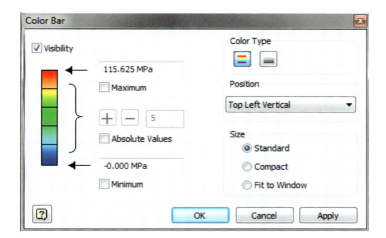

Absolute Values, when checked, displays all result values in absolute values and the color bar reflects those values.

 When **Absolute Values** is checked, the negative values for the maximum and minimum thresholds are invalid.

 The numbers of the color legend can only be changed when **Contour Shading** is selected. **Smooth Shading** by default will use **Maximum**.

Beam and node labels

These help with visually identifying specific nodes and beams by displaying labels, as illustrated below

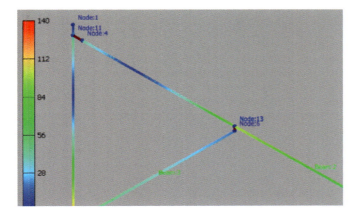

Display results

Here you can decide whether you want display smooth, contour and no results display

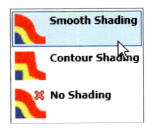

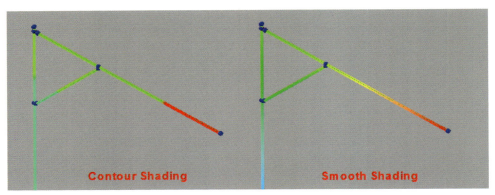

Probe Labels

Displays the user defined probe labels

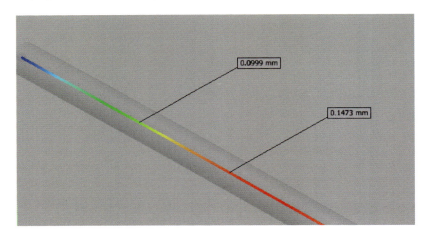

Adjust displacement display

Here you can adjust the scale of the results to obtain a better indication of whether boundary conditions applied are correct.

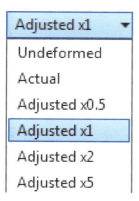

 Adjust the scale so that the deformation is visible before selecting **Animate results**, as animations without visible deformation are less visual.

Max and min values

Displays the maximum and minimum values, for the selected results type, aiding in locating their positions on the model, as illustrated below.

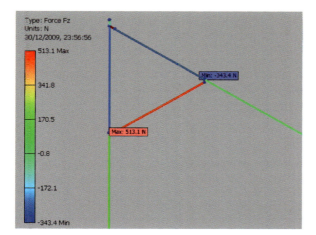

Boundary conditions

Displays all the loads and constraints applied on the model

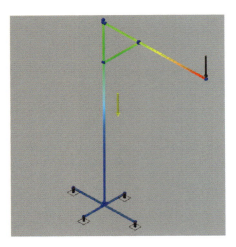

Local systems

Displays the local coordinate system for all beams

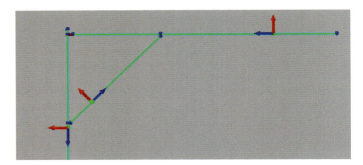

Load values

Displays load value associated with all the loads applied on the model.

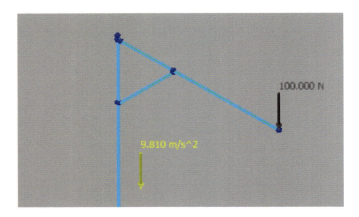

Boundary conditions need to be active in order to be able to see load values.

Publish tab

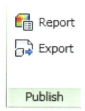

Report

Export

Publish

Report

Autodesk Inventor – in addition to standard html format – now lets you create reports in mhtml (single web page) and rich text formats (word documents), making it very easy to customize the reports to specific requirements.

 Microsoft Word is required to generate the RTF file.

In addition to being able to customize settings using the **General**, **Properties** and **Simulation** tabs from the **Report Generator** dialogue box, there are now more settings within the **Format** tab.

Use Dynamic Content - Select this to include size buttons for image width and buttons that you can click to collapse or expand the associated sections.

 Not available for the RTF format

Create OLE Link - Select to create an OLE link from the model browser to the report. The report icon displays under the **Third Party** folder in the model browser. To edit the report, double-click the icon or right-click and select **Edit**.

Frame Analysis Report

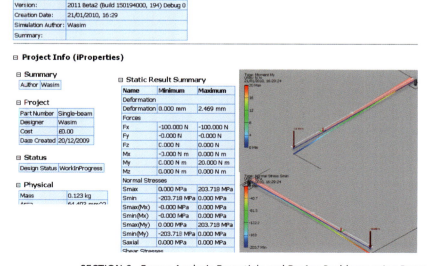

Export

Autodesk Inventor also allows to export frame analysis data to Autodesk Robot Structural analysis 2011 data in RTD file format.

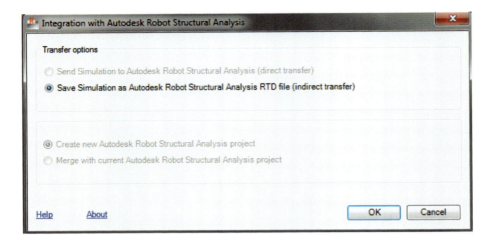

 Only available if an active Robot Structural Analysis license is installed.

The RTD file contains all defined loads, constraints, rigid links, releases, beam materials and beam sections.

The following export options are available:

- Save the simulation as an RTD file.

- **Send Simulation to Autodesk Robot Structural Analysis** – Directly creates a calculation model in Autodesk Robot Structural Analysis based on the current frame analysis data in Autodesk Inventor.

- **Create New Autodesk Robot Structural Analysis project**.

- **Merge with current Autodesk Robot Structural Analysis project**.

 Further details on **Export** are available in Autodesk Inventor Simulation **Help** menu

Frame Analysis Settings tab

Frame Analysis
Settings

Settings

Allows the predefinition of settings for current and preceding analyzes

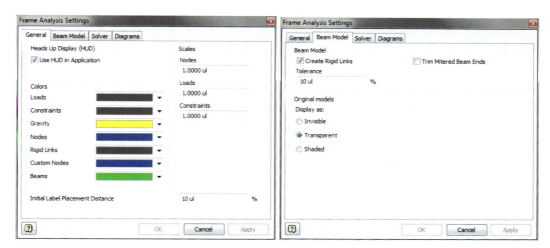

Use HUD in Application – Checked by default. Uncheck if you want to use the dialogue boxes for editing and creating boundary conditions etc.

 While creating boundary conditions, with HUD active, you can right-click and select **More Options**. This will allow you to edit using dialogue boxes.

Colors – Here you can define specific colors for loads constraints, nodes etc

Scales – Here you can alter the visual scale of the nodes, loads and constraints.

Beam Model – This is the tolerance that dictates whether a rigid link will be created between the beams that are not connected. The default value is 2%. When the distance between two beams is smaller than the sizes of sections multiplied by this tolerance, a rigid link connection is created via the shortest distance between nearest nodes. You can specify any value between -100% and 500%, with a negative value meaning that the beams needs be intersecting for a rigid link to be created.

Rigid Links - If selected will create rigid links between beams that have gaps.

Trim Mitered Beam Ends - When selected, the overlaps are trimmed during automatic model conversion

Original Models – Hear you can define how the original models appear in frame analysis. By default, the original models are set to transparent.

CHAPTER 14
The Frame Analysis Environment

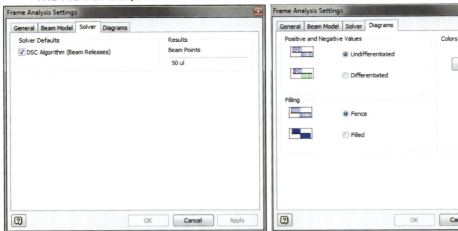

Solver Defaults - DSC Algorithm (Beam Releases) should be checked if the structure contains beam releases. The algorithm carries out the following operations:

1. A new node is generated in the structure (during the structure model generation).
2. The input element with the release is modified in such a way that the new node takes the place of the old one in the element (the old node remains in other structure elements).
3. Between the old and the new node, the program creates the so called DSC element; see the image on the next page.

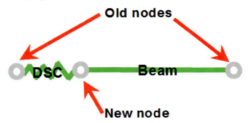

Results – Here you can specify number of beam points that are calculated by solving; this basically splits the beam into smaller linear beam elements. Any value between 5 and 1000 can be specified, with 50 being the default. This value can become important when analyzing a curved beam as the software will need to split the beam into lots of smaller linear elements to provide accurate results, as the software does not support curved beam elements.

Positive and Negative Values – Can specify how positive and negative values are visually displayed

- **Undifferentiated** – No to differentiation between positive and negative values
- **Differentiated** – Shows positive and negative values

Filling – Here you can specify how the diagrams will be filled

- **Fence** – Uses a fence-style shading to display the diagram
- **Filled** – Displays the diagram as completely shaded/filled

Colors – Select to change the colors of loads and stresses displayed in the graphic diagrams.

DP13 – Frame Analysis Using Content Centre Structures

Structural design of Aerospace Maintenance Platform
(Design Problem Courtesy of Planet Platforms Ltd)

Key features and workflows introduced in this design problem

	Key Features/Workflows
1	Content centre frames converted to beam elements
2	Tolerance settings – used to create rigid links automatically
3	Pinned constraints and continuous loading
4	Change material and beam properties

Introduction

Planet Platforms, established since 1977, is a leading manufacturer and distributor of work place access solutions. Ranging from podium steps to award-winning intelligent platforms, their access solutions have been keeping people safe for the past 30 years. Through a process of communication, site surveys, CAD rendered visuals and proven manufacturing, Plant Platform delivers the end result - a platform that is safe, reliable and perfectly suited for the application.

Some of their prestigious clients include Rolls Royce, Thomas Cook, the Orient Express, the Royal Albert Hall, ICI Chemicals, Shell Offshore and the National Trust

CHAPTER 15
DP13 – Frame Analysis Using Content Centre Structures

Above is a picture of platform that is used by Rolls Royce personal to carry out essential maintenance work. The platform is constructed from mild steel and is to be designed such that the platform, including steps, can withstand the load of two people including their maintenance equipment and other essential components.

To this effect a total load of 250Kg will be used to determine;

1. The maximum bending stress in the platform under normal operating conditions.
2. The maximum deflection in the platform.
3. The factor of safety (F.O.S).

With

4. Maximum deflection not to be above 5 mm.
5. Minimum F.O.S of 4.
6. Material construction to be limited to aluminum or mild steel
7. Frame tube construction to be used from Standard ISO Content Centre

Workflow of Design Problem 13

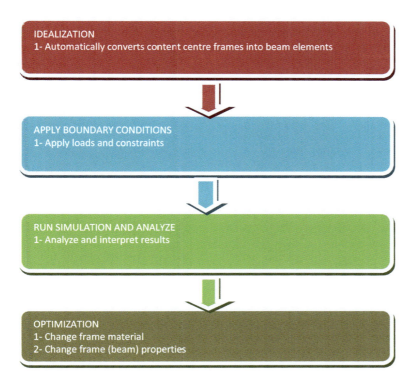

IDEALIZATION
1- Automatically converts content centre frames into beam elements

APPLY BOUNDARY CONDITIONS
1- Apply loads and constraints

RUN SIMULATION AND ANALYZE
1- Analyze and interpret results

OPTIMIZATION
1- Change frame material
2- Change frame (beam) properties

Idealization

Frame Analysis within Inventor Simulation automatically converts frame/channels created from both Content Centre and Frame Generator. All other components will be not be converted and therefore are not included in the analysis. Note: if neither Content Centre nor Frame Generator is used to create any content then no frame or channels will be idealized into beam elements.

1.   Open *Platform*.iam

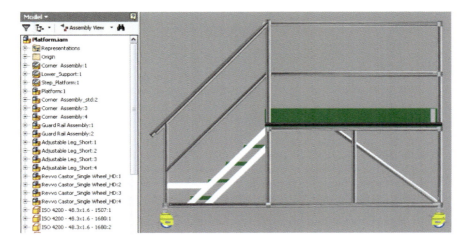

Now we can begin the second stage of the analysis of applying boundary conditions.

CHAPTER 15
DP13 – Frame Analysis Using Content Centre Structures
Boundary conditions

2.   Select **Environments** tab > **Frame Analysis**

3.   Select **Create Simulation** > Select **Model State** tab > Select **Main-Structure** for **Level of Detail** > Click **OK**

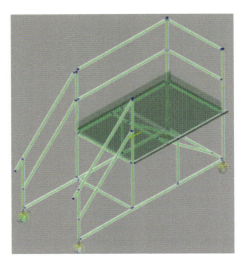

This will idealize all the content centre frames into beam elements and exclude all the remaining parts/assemblies from the analysis (shown transparently).

The steps and supporting frames are not included in this beam analysis, as the assembly was not part of the level of detail.

It is also important to note that, as the frames where connected via tee-connectors -which are not included in the analysis - there will be gaps between the ends of the beams, shown below.

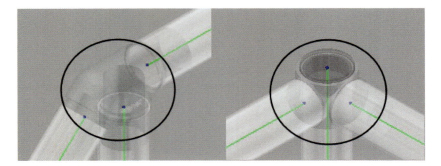

To connect these beams via rigid links, the tolerance needs to increased.

4.   Select **Frame Analysis Settings** > Select the **Beam Model** tab > Change **tolerance** setting from 2% to 50% > Click **OK**

5.   Select **Update**

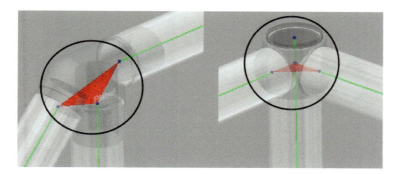

All the beams at the tee connections are now connected via rigid links. This can be verified by simply looking at all the connection points. For large modes this can be tedious and, hence, in these situations it would be quicker to do a modal analysis to check whether all beams are connected by analyzing the deformation results. The gravity is acting in the wrong direction so first we need to specify gravity to act downwards.

6.   Right click **Gravity** in the browser > Select **Edit** > Change **Direction** to positive X direction > Click **OK**

Next, we are going to apply the constraints and loads so we can determine structural integrity of the platform when carrying two people with necessary maintenance equipment.

7.   Select **Pinned Constraint** > Right click > Select **More Options** > Select node at the bottom near the wheels to define **Origin** of the constraint > Select **Apply**

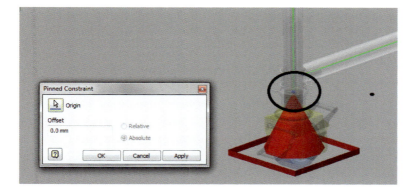

8. Repeat step 7 for creating pinned constraint at the other three wheels > Click **OK** once the last node has been selected.

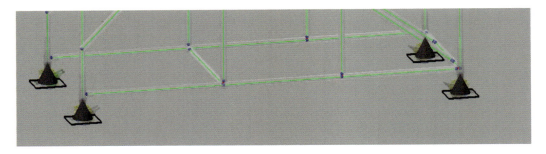

The platform needs to withstand the load of two maintenance workers, including the weight of the tools, components etc. This equates to a weight of 125Kg/person. So the total load the platform needs to withstand is 2500, using the value of 10 m/s^2 for gravity

$$Total\ Load = Weight\ of\ person\ x\ number\ of\ people\ x\ gravity$$

As the platform deck is supported by the frames directly beneath it, this load will be distributed evenly across all these frames. The load we will use is the continuous load N/mm .To calculate this value, we determine the total length of all the frames directly supporting the platform deck and then divide the total load by the total length of the frames. This will be a good estimate to determine the weight of the two people, in the absence of the platform deck not being analyzed.

$$Continuous\ Load = \frac{2500}{6.6} = 378N/m = 0.378N/mm$$

9. Select **Continuous Load** > Right click > Select **More Options** > Select beam as shown > Specify **0.378**N/mm for load value > Select **Apply**

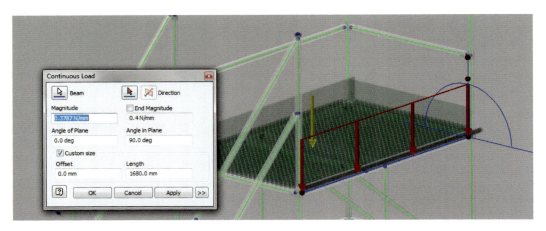

10. Repeat step 9 for the other four beam elements directly under the platform deck > Click **OK**

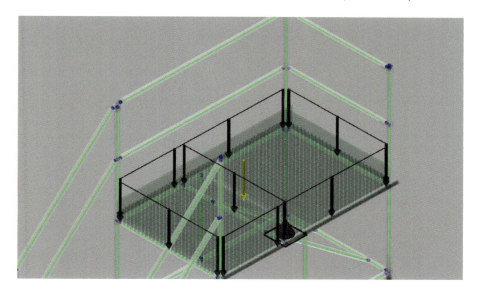

📝 There should be five Continuous loads in the browser.

Run simulation and analyze

11. Select **Simulate**

12. Select Adjust x 1 for **Displacement Display** > Select **Smax Normal Stress**

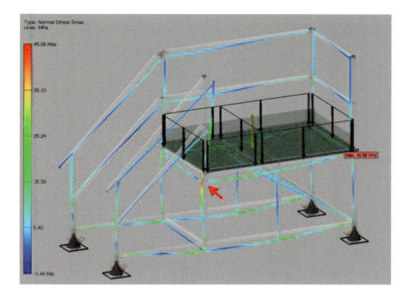

There are two maximum stresses, one at the front, illustrated by the arrow, and one at the back, shown by max value, the maximum deflection being 1.464mm. We will now reanalyze the platform but this time will include additional steps and see whether they have an effect on the overall structural integrity of the platform.

13. Right click Simulation:1 > Select **Copy Simulation**

14. Right click Simulation:2 > Select **Edit Simulation**

15. Select **Model State** tab > Select **Master** for **Level of Detail**

The warning refers to that the model may need to be updated

16. Click **OK** > Cancel Warning

The warning refers to that some beam elements have a zero value for torsional modulus

17. Select **Frame Analysis Settings** > Select **Beam Model** tab > Select **Invisible** for the original models not included in the analysis > Click **OK**

18. Select **Simulate** to rerun the analysis again.

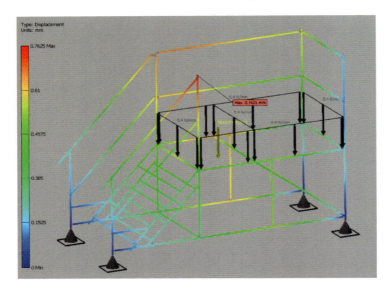

The maximum deflection has reduced by half to 0.7614mm

 Select **Display Load values** to visually display load values. This helps to see whether any loads have been applied incorrectly.

19. Select **Smax Normal Stress** > Unselect **Display of Load values** and **Boundary Conditions** > Select **Color Bar** > Unselect **Maximum Value** > Specify **30** as **new Maximum Value** > Click **OK**

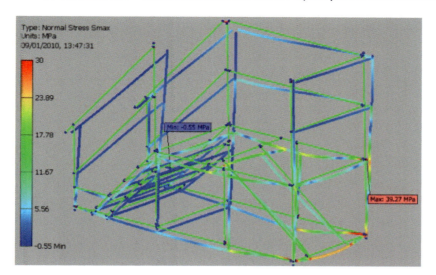

Although the maximum stress value has reduced, it is worth noting that the stress due to bending at the front has considerably reduced by adding the steps structure. We can now confidently say the steps structure is fundamental to the structural integrity of the platform. You will also note that the axial, shear, torsional stresses are insignificant compared to the stresses caused by bending. This can be investigated by looking at different stress plots using axial, torsional, and shear stress results. Based on the maximum stress value the minimum factor of safety is

$$\textit{Factor of Safety} = \frac{\text{Yield Stress}}{\text{Operationl Stress}} = \frac{207}{39.27} = 5.27$$

This meets the minimum design F.O.S of **4**.

Optimization

As the structure is made from mild steel, we would like to investigate whether the platform was to be constructed from aluminum. In Frame Analysis, it is very easy to multi-select all frames and override material specified within Content Centre. This is ideal to check the suitability of different materials before changing the material via Content Centre – which can be tedious, especially when you have a lot of frames/components.

20. Right Click Simulation:2 > Select **Copy Simulation**

21. Select **Material** from the **Beams** panel of the **Frame Analysis** tab

22. Highlight all beams > Select **Customize** > Change **Material** to **Aluminium-6061** > Click **OK**

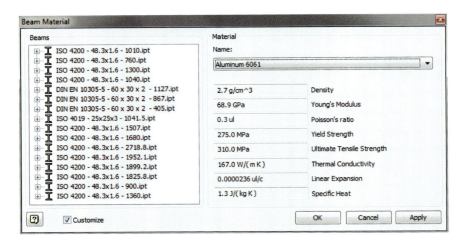

23. Select **Simulate** > Select **Actual** for **Displacement Display** > Select **Color bar** > Unselect **Maximum** value > Specify **1** > Click **OK**

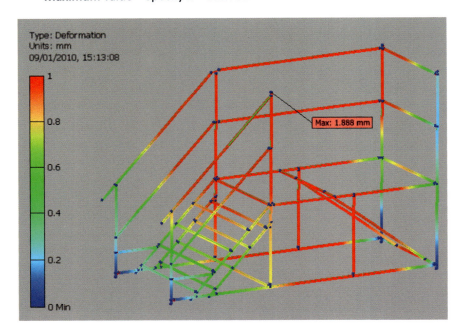

The max deflection has more than doubled to 1.888mm; this is due the fact that aluminum is more flexible than steel. Although the deflection has increased, it is negligible and insignificant in terms of the overall dimensions of the platform. Another thing to note that maximum stress has reduced slightly to 34.48MPa because aluminum has a higher yield stress value. The F.O.S now becomes

$$Factor\ of\ Safety = \frac{Yield\ Stress}{Operationl\ Stress} = \frac{275}{34.48} = 7.96$$

As the factor of safety is almost twice the design F.O.S, a value of 4, we will investigate using a smaller tube with twice the thickness; tube ISO 4200 33.7 X 3.2. Again, it is considerable task to change the frames for the purposes of frame analysis. Here, we will consider overriding the key mechanical properties of the original tube with those of the proposed tube, illustrated below.

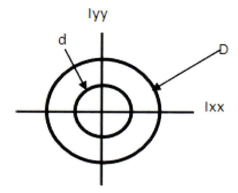

Note calculations are in mm for the following:-

$$Area = \pi(D^2 - d^2)/4 \quad \& \quad Ixx = Iyy = \pi(D^4 - d^4)/64 \quad \& \quad Ixx + Iyy = Izz$$

$$Area = \pi(33.7^2 - 27.3^2)/4 = 306.619 \text{mm}^2$$

$$Ixx = Iyy = \pi(D^4 - d^4)/64 = \pi(33.7^4 - 27.3^4)/64 = 36046.565$$

We will override the default values with the above to represent new tube ISO4200 33.7X3.2, in addition to the Centroid (16.85mm) and Wz values.

24. Right Click Simulation:3 > Select **Copy Simulation**

25. Expand the Beams node > Select beams 1 to 27 > Right Click > Select **Beam Properties**

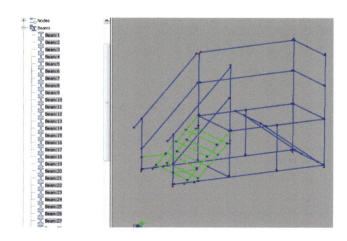

We are not including the step structure as they are constructed from box sections and not tubes.

26. Highlight all beams > Select **Customize** > Specify new calculated values > Click **OK**

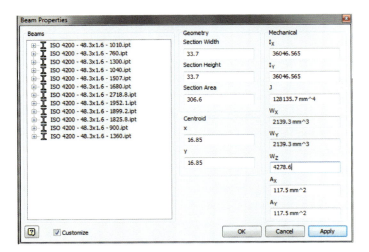

Will leave Ax and Ay values as we are only interested in the maximum stress due to bending

27. Select **Simulate** > Accept warning

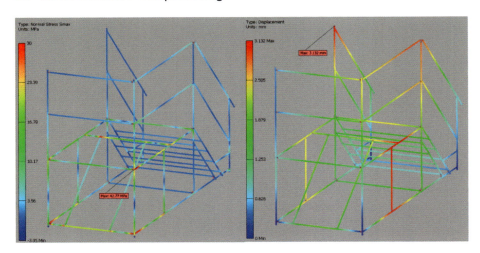

The results show that the deflection has increased to 3.132 mm and maximum stress to 42.77MPa. Value may differ slightly

Now taking this new value the F.O.S now is 4.5

$$Factor\ of\ Safety = \frac{Yield\ Stress}{Operationl\ Stress} = \frac{275}{42.77} = 6.4$$

As both value are within the specified design criteria we can safely replace the existing tubes ISO 4200 43.8 X 1.6, with tube ISO 4200 33.7 X 3.2.

28. Select **Finish Frame Analysis** > Close File

DP14 – Frame Analysis Using Frame Generator Structures

Analysis of an Escalator Support Structure
(Design Problem courtesy of KONE plc)

Key features and workflows introduced in this design problem

	Key Features/Workflows
1	Frames , created using Frame Generator, converted to beam elements
2	Tolerance settings – used to create rigid links automatically
3	Custom constraints and multiple forces
4	Beam diagram, detail and scales

Introduction

KONE plc is a world's leading manufacturer of escalators and caters for various markets including retail, infrastructure, leisure and offices. Retail markets include supermarkets and shopping malls, whereas the Infrastructure market serves underground tubes, train stations and airports. Kone support their customers every step of the way, from design, manufacturing, and installation to maintenance and modernization.

CHAPTER 16
DP14– Frame Analysis Using Frame Generator Structures

Above is a picture of a typical passenger escalator, within a shopping mall. The escalator design goes through intensive tests to make sure they are safe. A typical requirement in escalator design is to make sure that the support structure, holding the escalator, can hold the weight of passengers and of key components including steps and balustrade etc.

In this example we will determine the strength of the structure in relation to the weight of the structure, passengers and balustrade;

1. The structure weight is based on density of material, which is mild steel.
2. For the passenger load, a value of 200kg or 2000N will be used.
3. The weight of the balustrade will be applied as a continuous load of 1.2N/mm.

Note: In practice a typical escalator can go through up to thirty different load cases to fully validate the designs.

The design requirements are:

4. Maximum deflection not to exceed 3mm
5. Minimum factor of safety (FOS) to be 4

Workflow of Design Problem 14

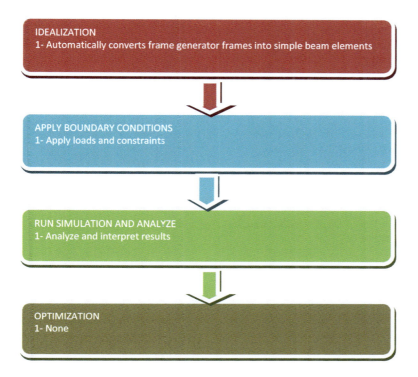

Idealization

As mentioned in the previous example, idealization is done automatically by converting frames created by Frame generator and Content Centre into simple line beam elements. It is important to note, however, that frame analysis cannot be used if neither Content Centre nor Frame Generator is used to create the frames and channels, as frame analysis will have nothing to analyze.

1.   Open Kone.iam

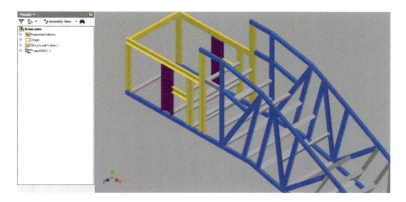

Now we can begin the second stage of the analysis of applying boundary conditions.

Boundary conditions

2. Select **Design** tab > Select **Frame Analysis**

3. Select **Create Simulation** > Click **OK**

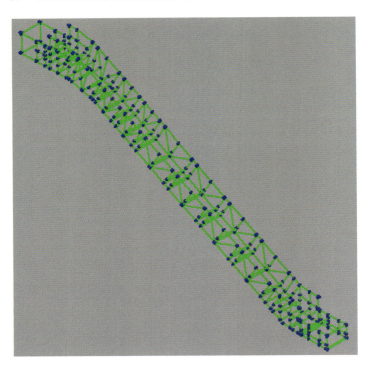

📝 This takes a little while as a total of 230 beams and 239 rigid links are created

💡 Modal analysis is a very quick way to easily investigate unconnected beams, especially when the model has a large number of beams. This will help in identifying the need to create rigid links manually or automatically by increasing the beam model tolerance.
Note only constraints are required to run a modal analysis.

4. Select **Frame Analysis** Settings > Change Rigid Links color to red > Change scale of **Nodes** to 1 > Change scale of **Constraints** to 1 > Click **OK**

In the following steps, fixed constraints will be applied to top end of the escalator structure.

5. Select **Fixed Constraint** > Right click > Select **More Options** >Select the parent node as shown > Select **Apply**

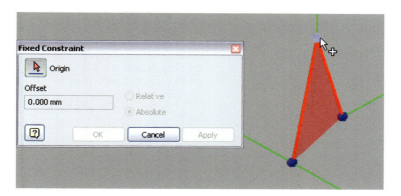

Only the parent node, within the rigid links, is selectable

6. Repeat step 5 to apply more constraints on the other locations defined below

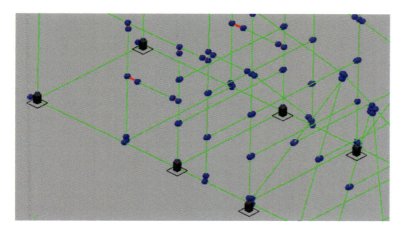

Now we need to apply floating pin constraints at the V frame junctions as indicated below

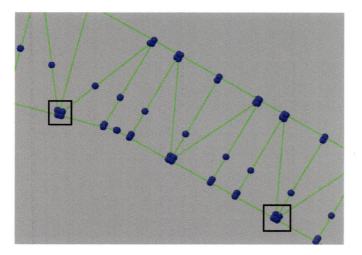

The constraints are to be applied at each alternating V junction on both sides of the structure on the incline of the escalator support structure. However, as we cannot apply rotational constraints, including pinned and floating constraints, on parent nodes of rigid links, we will apply a custom constraint simulated as a floating constraint. The floating constraint will restrict the motion of the escalator in the vertical direction only

7. Select **Custom Constraint** > Select **Uplift none** for all displacements except the Y axis > Select **Uplift none** for all rotations > Select A**pply**

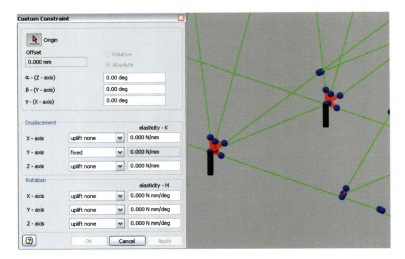

8. Repeat step 7 for applying custom constraints on the other locations illustrated below

Do not close the dialogue box once all eight custom constraints have been created.

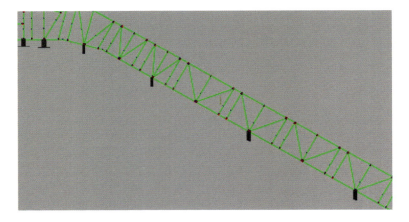

Finally, the custom constraint needs to be applied at the bottom end of the escalator and again the constraints should be such that the escalator is restricted in the vertical direction only.

9. Select the parent nodes of the rigid links at the following locations to create custom constraints > Click **OK** once all six constraints have been created

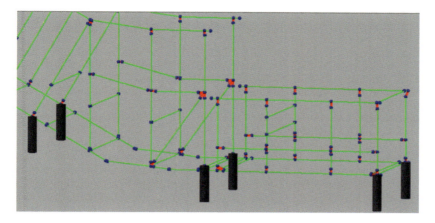

As all constraints have now been applied, the loads need to be defined on the support structure.

The first load to be taken into account is of the balustrade weight, as shown above, which will be applied as a continuous load of 1.2 N/mm

10. Select **Continuous load** > Right click > Select **More Options** > Specify 1.2N/mm for **Magnitude** > Select the beam as shown > Select **Apply**

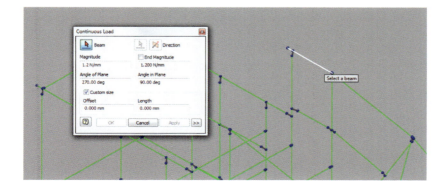

11. Repeat step 10 until all beams on the top, on both sides, have been selected as shown below
> Click **OK**

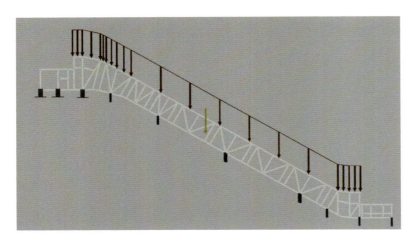

Run simulation and analyze

12. Select **Simulate** > Cancel Warning

13. Select **Display** > Deselect **Boundary Conditions** > Select **Maximum Value**

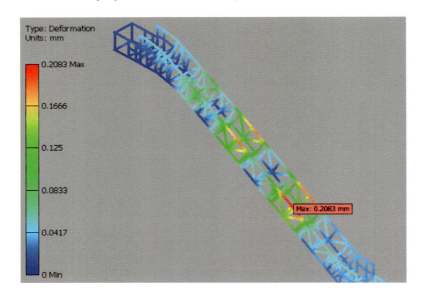

The maximum deflection is only 0.2 mm under the balustrade load and is well below the limit. We will next look at the maximum bending stress in the structure.

14. Select **Frame Analysis** Settings > Change scale of **Nodes** to 0.1 > Click **OK**

15. Select **Smax Normal Stress** > Select **Color Bar** > Unselect **Maximum Value** >Specify **6** as new **Maximum Value** > Select **Absolute Values** > Click **OK**

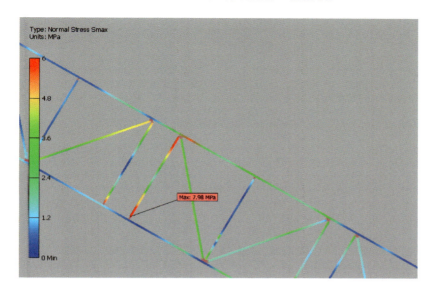

Value may differ slightly

Next, we are going to look at the bending Stresses across the lower long beam of the escalator.

16. Select **Diagram** > **Activate Selected Beam** > Select the beam as shown

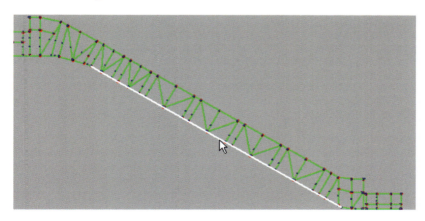

17. Select **Maximum Smax** > Click **OK**

18. Select **Frame Analysis Settings** > Select **Diagrams** tab > Select the **Differentiated** and **Filled** option > Select **Colors** > Select **Red** for **Smax** > Click **OK** twice

19. Right Click Diagram:1 > Select **Diagram Scales** > Change **Normal Stresses** to 0.00500 MPa/mm > Click **OK**

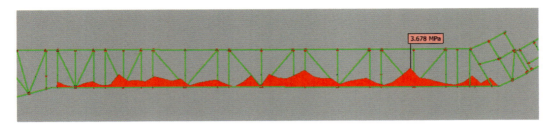

Value may differ slightly

Beam Detail will provide a more comprehensive summary of results, including the reactions of the selected beam.

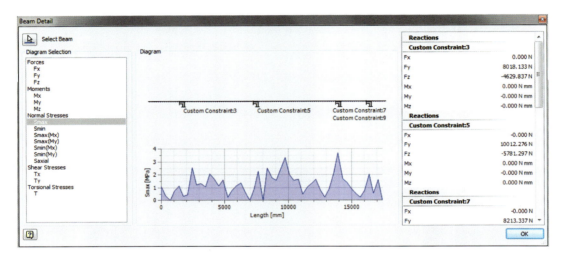

A typical escalator analysis can have up to 30 load cases, including passenger and step load cases. To analysis of all these load cases is beyond the scope of this exercise and therefore only the passenger load case will be considered in addition to the balustrade weight (including the weight of the escalator structure). Each step of the escalator needs to carry two people, including any extra weight that they may be carrying, for example shopping goods etc. Therefore, the weight to be used for the purposes of analysis is 200 kg (or 2000 N) per person.

DP14– Frame Analysis Using Frame Generator Structures

The load of the passenger is transferred to structure via escalator tracks, as shown below.

The tracks are positioned 200 mm from the sides and therefore the forces need to be applied on the cross members 200 mm offset from either end. The length of these cross member is ≈ 1540 mm, which means the values for offsetting the forces will be 200mm and 1340mm.

20. Right Click Simulation:1 > Select **Copy Simulation**

21. Select **Force** > Right click > Select **More Options** >Select **2000** for **Magnitude** > Select beam as shown > Select **1340**mm for **Offset** > Select **Apply**

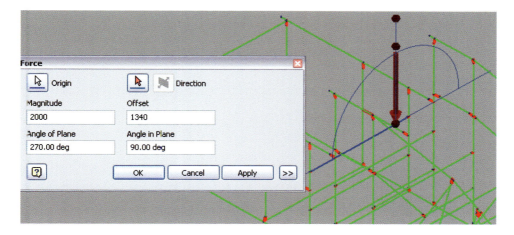

22. Select same beam again > Select **200**mm for **Offset** > Click **Apply**

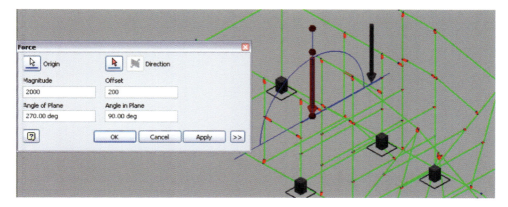

CHAPTER 16

DP14– Frame Analysis Using Frame Generator Structures

23. Repeat steps **20-21** for all cross member beams on the escalator

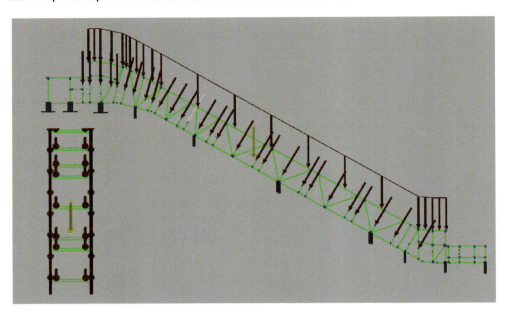

 60 forces in total are created

 The forces on the incline are @ 30° to the vertical such as **Angle of Plane** is 240°

 The four forces on the top between the horizontal and the incline, as shown below, have an **Angle of Plane** value of 255°

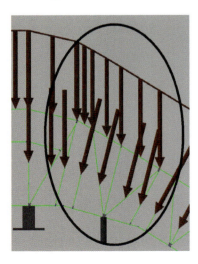

24. Select **Simulate**

The maximum value has now increased from 0.2 mm to 1mm.

25. Select S_{max} **Normal Stress** > Select **Color Bar** > Unselect **Maximum Value** >Specify **15** as new **Maximum value** > Select **Absolute Values** > Click **OK**

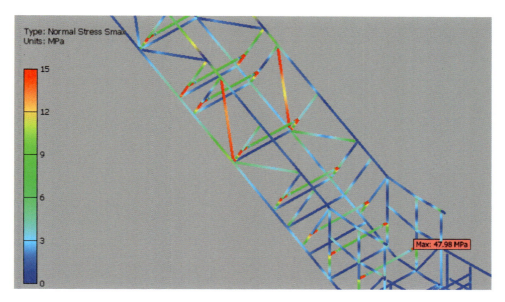

Value may differ slightly

The maximum stress value has increased from 10.95MPa to 47.98MPa. Based on this new value the minimum factor of safety is

$$Factor\ of\ Safety = \frac{\text{Yield Stress}}{\text{Operationl Stress}} = \frac{207}{48} = 4.3$$

A typical escalator, as mentioned earlier, will go through several more load case analyses.

26. Select **Finish Frame Analysis** > Close File

DP15 – Frame Analysis Using Advance Settings

Analysis of an Offshore Container
(Design Problem courtesy of Swire Oilfield Services Ltd)

Key features and workflows introduced in this design problem

	Key Features/Workflows
1	Rigid Links to simulate Slings
2	Modifying and Creating Rigid Links
3	Custom Constraints with Stiffness Properties
4	Rigid Link Releases

Introduction

Swire Oilfield Services, part of the global conglomerate, the Swire group, is the world's largest supplier of specialist offshore cargo carrying units to the global energy industry and is a leading supplier of cargo carrying solutions, modular systems, offshore aviation services and fluid management.

SECTION 6 - Frame Analysis Essentials and Design Problems using Beam Elements

CHAPTER 17
DP15– Frame Analysis Using Advance Settings

Established in 1979, Swire Oilfield Services provides the largest hire fleet worldwide. Its in-house engineering capability allows the company to design and manufacture customized equipment. The company supplies tailored modular workspace systems and services to the marine and energy industries.

Swire Oilfield Services' comprehensive fluid management services save its customers time and money and minimizes health and safety concerns both on and offshore. Through its fully certified and approved offshore aviation services, Swire Oilfield Services plays a crucial role in the efficient operations of offshore helicopters.

Operating in 31 countries, Swire Oilfield Services has a team of over 750 staff in 36 bases around the globe. The company has a presence in all major oil and gas regions with large operations in Northern Europe, The Americas, Africa, Asia Pacific and Australia

Swire Oilfield Services design, manufacture and physically test all of their offshore containers to meet DET NORSKE VERITAS (DNV for short) 2.7.1 Standard. Two of the tests they have to meet is the 4 and 2 Point Lift. Using FEA analysis the primary structure (excluding side wall and floor etc) of the component is either modeled as shells or beams, in this example we will use beams. To simulate the realistic behavior of the container as much as possible the lifting sets (slings) will be included and again modeled as beams.

In this design problem we will simulate a 4 Point and 2 Lift test for one of Swire's Unit within Inventor Simulation under DNV guidelines. The offshore container needs to lift 65 tonnes and for the purposes of this exercise the material to be used is Mild Steel for the container.

Workflow of Design Problem 15

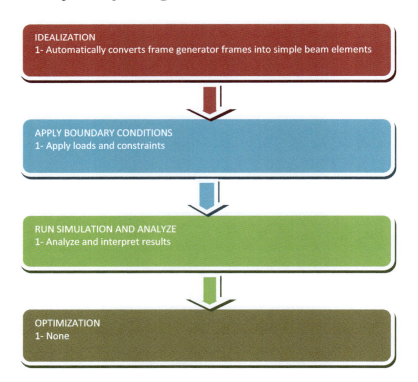

SECTION 6 - Frame Analysis Essentials and Design Problems using Beam Elements

Idealization

Idealization is done automatically by converting frames created by Frame generator and Content Centre into simple line beam elements. It is also worth noting that to reduce the complexity of rigid links, automatically created, is not to perform end treatments, via frame generator, prior to any frame analysis. As such in this example, unlike the previous example, majority of the frames are overlapping.

1. Open *Offshore-Container*.iam

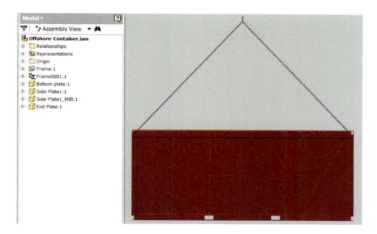

By further examining the model we can see that all frames are overlapping

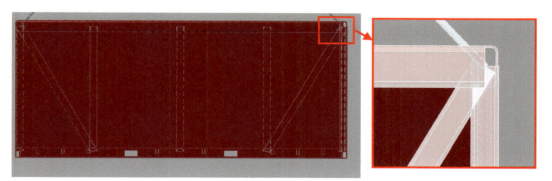

For the purposes of Frame Analysis performing end treatment, using Frame Generator, will have minimal impact on results.

Now we can begin the second stage of the analysis of applying boundary conditions.

Boundary conditions

2. Select **Design** tab > Select **Frame Analysis**

3. Select **Create Simulation** > For **Name** specify **4 Point Lift** > Click **OK**

CHAPTER 17

DP15– Frame Analysis Using Advance Settings

To be able to better see the beams and rigid links created change the visibility of original models from transparent to invisible, via Frame Analysis Settings. Rigid links are created as a result of specifying offset positions when placing content/structures using Frame Generator.

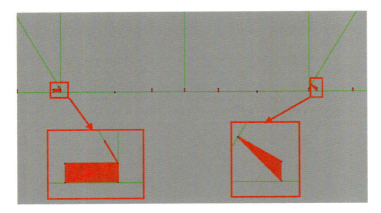

 If no offset positions are specified when placing content, via frame generator, then all beam elements will be connected. This also means there will be no gaps between beams, hence no rigid links will be automatically created, or needed.

The complexity of four of the rigid links created, two on each side, can be simplified by creating then manually, and suppressing the one's automatically created.

4. Select one of the rigid links in the graphics window as illustrated in above image > Right click > Select **Suppress**

Repeat step 4 for the remaining three rigid links. Four Rigid links will now be suppressed in the browser, under the Rigid Links heading. We are going to start to create manual rigid links, in the following steps, starting from the front end (the opening)

5. Select **Frame Analysis Settings** > Change Nodes Scales to **0.5** > Click **OK**

6. Select **Rigid Links** > Select top node for Parent and bottom node for child as indicated below > Click **Apply**. A rigid link will be created as shown by the red line below

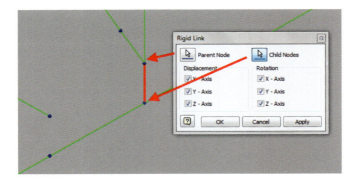

7. Now repeat step **6** to connect the two beam nodes in front > Click **Apply.** Another rigid link will be created as shown below

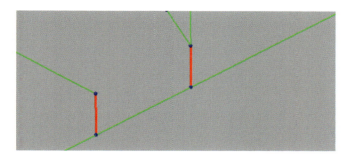

Now repeat step 6 to 7 for the other side. In the following steps we are going to create rigid links towards the back end of the container.

8. Select top node for Parent and bottom node for child as indicated below > Click **Apply.** A rigid link will be created as shown by the red line below

Now repeat step 8 for the other side. The following four simplified rigid links will be created (two on each side)

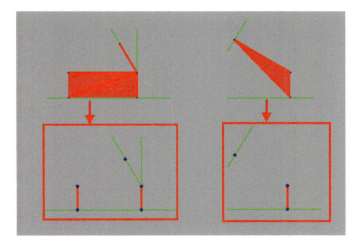

Now modify Gravity to point in the negative Z-direction. Now we are going to specify a pin constraint at top of the slings as in reality the slings are attached via a hook, which will allow rotation.

9. Right Click **Gravity** > Select **Edit** > Set Direction to **-Z** > Click **OK**

10. Select **Pin Constraint** > Select the node as shown > Click **OK**

💡 Select away from the node anywhere along a beam and then change Offset options to Relative. Depending on which end is 0 or 1, select either 0 or 1 to specify constraint at the end of the beam. This is quicker than trying to select the end node.

📝 Custom nodes cannot be created in space, hence the need to create this extra beam, as later in the exercise we will be using rigid links which will require a node in space.

11. Select **Fixed Constraint** > Select the top node as shown > Click **OK**

12. Select **Simulate** > Change **Adjustment Displacement Display** to **Actual**

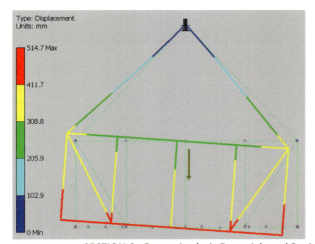

As you can see the maximum displacement value seems high under gravity load, indicating the model is unstable. In the following steps we will attempt to make the model stable by specifying custom constraints, at each corner of the container, with some stiffness value specified in two direction, not in the direction of the loading.

13. Select **Custom Constraint** > Specify the following values

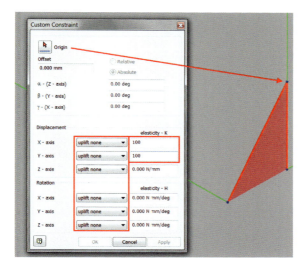

For Inventor Frame Analysis a value of 100N/mm provides a stable model by restraining two translational directions on all corners of the frame. This technique is widely used when analyzing containers using any FEA software, with the only difference being the value used. You can experiment with different values to simulate physical testing results

14. Select **Origin** > Select the Parent node, as indicated above > Click **Apply**

15. Repeat step 14 for the other three corners.

16. Select **Simulate**

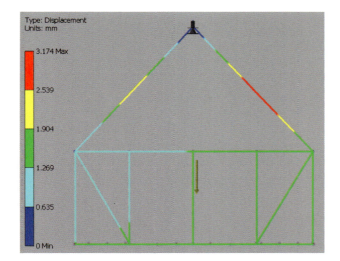

SECTION 6 - Frame Analysis Essentials and Design Problems using Beam Elements

CHAPTER 17
DP15– Frame Analysis Using Advance Settings

As the model is now more stable, we now need to determine the 4 point and 2 point lifting loads to test the strength of the container using the following data;

Main data for calculations	
Max. gross mass (R)	25000kg
Payload	18500kg
Tare mass	6500kg
Sling leg angle	45°
Enhancement factor	1.104

4 Point Lifting Load

Load on structure   F=(2.5xR)g = (2.5x25000)x9.81 = **613,125N**

2 Point Lifting Load

Load on structure   F=(1.5xR)g = (1.5x25000)x9.81 = **367,875N**

Initially we are going to test the structure using the 4 point lifting load value of 613,125N. As the container at the bottom is supported by 10 cross-members, excluding the outer members, we need to spread this load uniformly across all members using Continuous Load. To calculate this value, we determine the total length of all the frames directly supporting the floor of the container and then divide the total load by the total length of the frames. In this example the length of the frames supporting the floor of the container are 2750mm.

$$\text{Continuous Load} = \frac{613125}{2750 \times 10} = 22.295\text{N/mm}$$

17. Select **Continuous load** > Right click > Select **More Options** > Specify **613125/27500** for **Magnitude** > Select the beam as shown > Select **Apply**

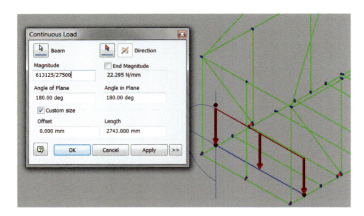

Used a value of 2750mm as an approx value for the purposes of calculating Load

18. Repeat step 17 until all the other nine beams on the bottom have been selected > Click **OK**

Run simulation and analyze

19. Select **Simulate**

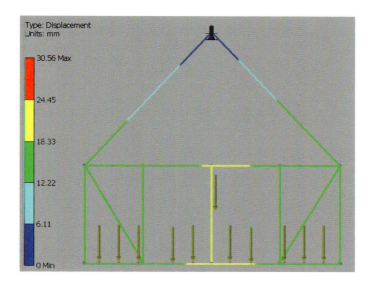

As we applied custom constraints at each corner of the frame we need to check whether they had any impact on the results.

20. Select **Custom Constraint:1** > Right Click > Select **Reactions**

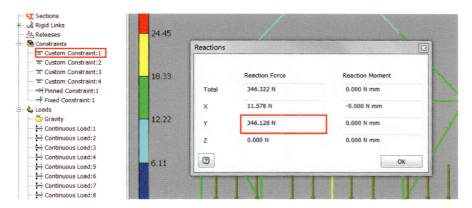

The maximum value 346.128N in the Y direction is small possibly suggesting a small person is leaning against the corner to stop the container swinging outwards. Note the reaction in the Z direction is zero as we did not want to restrain in the direction of the loading.

21. Click **OK**

22. Now select **Pinned Constraint:1** > Right Click > Select **Reactions**

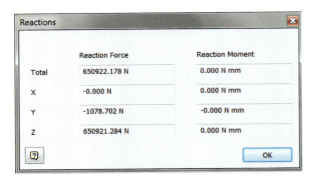

The Z value is higher than 613,125N as the extra value is due to the dead weight of the container.

The following value is achieved by running the simulation again with Gravity suppressed.

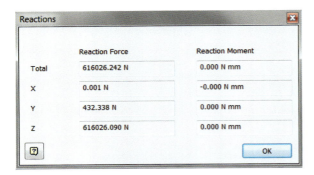

The above value of 616,026N indicates that applying custom constraints has minimal impact on results. The slight difference in the value is due to approximating the length of the cross members.

23. Select **Probe** > Select the node as shown

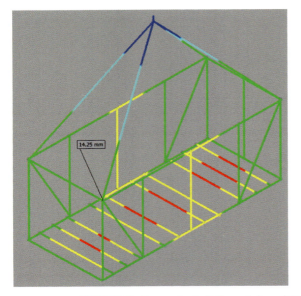

SECTION 6 - Frame Analysis Essentials and Design Problems using Beam Elements

This indicates that the sling has extended by 14.25mm. This is based on the slings being made out of Mild Steel. If this value is higher than physical tests then we can make the slings out of rigid material. This can be achieved by creating a new material and specify the maximum young's modulus, within Frame Analysis, which happens to be 1300GPa

Properties	Values
Density	1 g/cm^3
Young's Modulus	1300GPa
Poisson's Ration	0.3
Yield Strength	1000MPa
UTS	2000MPa

 Other values are not important as they relate to thermal analysis and can be left as zero values if you prefer.

Alternatively we can use rigid links to simulate slings, which will be used in this example

24. Expand the Beams heading in the browser > Select the following beams (the slings) > Right click > Select **Suppress**

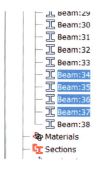

25. Select **Frame Analysis Settings** > Change Constraints Scales to **0.5** > Click **OK**

26. Select **Custom Nodes** > Right click > Select **More Options** > Select position of node on beam as shown > Change to **Relative** option > Specify **0.98** > Click **Apply**

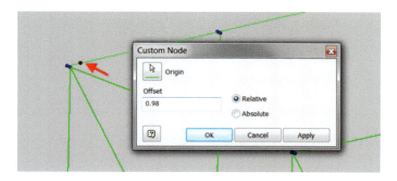

CHAPTER 17
DP15– Frame Analysis Using Advance Settings

27. Now select other side of same beam > Change to **Relative** option > Specify **0.02** > Click **Apply**

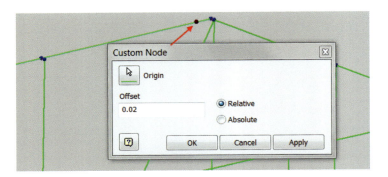

28. Repeat step 26 to 27 for the beam on the opposite side

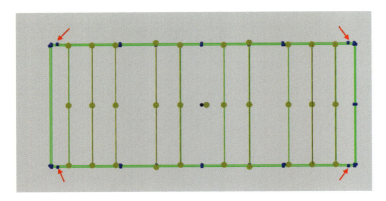

29. Select **Rigid Links** from the **Connections** panel

30. Select the node as shown for Parent Node > Unselect Rotational about **X-Axis** and **Y-Axis** (Global)

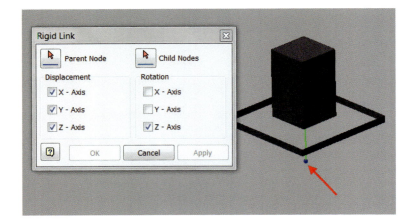

31. Select the four newly created custom nodes for Child Nodes > Click **OK**

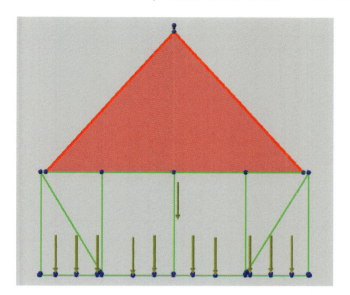

32. Select **Pin Constraint** > Select the top node of the Rigid Link (The pin constraint may have been removed as it may be connected to one of the beams when initially placed, and now suppressed)

33. Select **Simulate**

CHAPTER 17
DP15– Frame Analysis Using Advance Settings

The sling now only extends by 2.66mm (create a probe by selecting one of the custom nodes created).

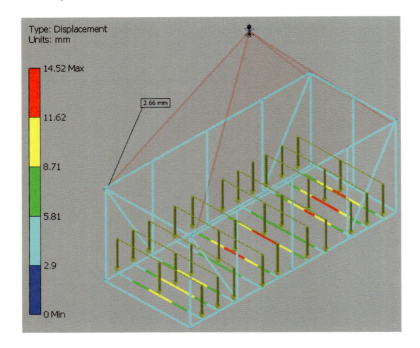

The maximum displacement has also reduced to 14.52mm.

34. Select **Smax Normal Stesses** > Select **Color Bar** > Deselect **Maximum** > Specify **150** > Select **Absolute Values** > Click **OK** > Deselect **Boundary Conditions**

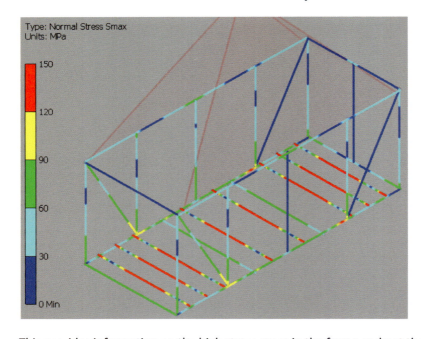

This provides information on the high stress areas in the frame and not the slings

Now in the following steps we are going to test the structure using the 2 point lifting load value of 367,875N

$$\text{Continuous Load} = \frac{367875}{2750 \times 10} = 13.377 \text{N/mm}$$

35. Select **Rigid Link:46** > Right click > Select **Edit** > Deselect two of the child nodes on the opposite diagonal ends >Select Rotational about **X-Axis** > Click **OK**

Fixing rotation about global X-Axis will make the model

36. Change the continuous load values to **13.377N/mm** for all 10 loads

37. **Select Simulate**

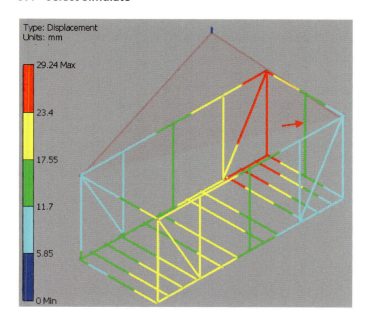

The displacement has now extended to 29.24mm. The unsymmetrical results are due to having a structural beam at one end, indicated by the arrow

38. Select **Smax Normal Stesses** > Select **Maximum Value**

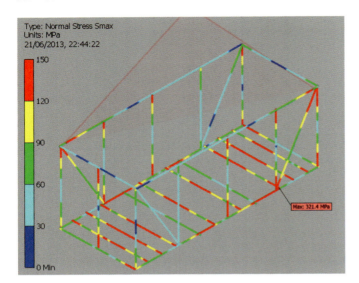

The maximum value of 321.4MPa is high which needs to be further investigated as in the event of the slings snapping can result in permanent deformation, obviously this depends on the yield limit of the material.

39. Select **Finish Frame Analysis** > Close File

Printed in Great Britain
by Amazon